D1142794

The
manic mum's
guide to
magnificent
parenting

The manic mum's guide to magnificent parenting

Allison Mitchell

HAY HOUSE

Australia • Canada • Hong Kong • India
South Africa • United Kingdom • United States

First published and distributed in the United Kingdom by:
Hay House UK Ltd, 292B Kensal Rd, London W10 5BE. Tel.: (44) 20
8962 1230; Fax: (44) 20 8962 1239. www.hayhouse.co.uk

Published and distributed in the United States of America by:
Hay House, Inc., PO Box 5100, Carlsbad, CA 92018-5100. Tel.: (1) 760
431 7695 or (800) 654 5126; Fax: (1) 760 431 6948 or (800) 650 5115.
www.hayhouse.com

Published and distributed in Australia by:
Hay House Australia Ltd, 18/36 Ralph St, Alexandria NSW 2015. Tel.:
(61) 2 9669 4299; Fax: (61) 2 9669 4144. www.hayhouse.co.au

Published and distributed in the Republic of South Africa by:
Hay House SA (Pty), Ltd, PO Box 990, Witkoppen 2068. Tel./Fax: (27)
11 467 8904. www.hayhouse.co.za

Published and distributed in India by:
Hay House Publishers India, Muskaan Complex, Plot No.3, B-2, Vasant
Kunj, New Delhi – 110 070. Tel.: (91) 11 4176 1620; Fax: (91) 11 4176
1630. www.hayhouse.co.in

Distributed in Canada by:
Raincoast, 9050 Shaughnessy St, Vancouver, BC V6P 6E5. Tel.: (1) 604
323 7100; Fax: (1) 604 323 2600

© Allison Mitchell, 2008

The moral rights of the author have been asserted.

All rights reserved. No part of this book may be reproduced by any
mechanical, photographic or electronic process, or in the form of a
phonographic recording; nor may it be stored in a retrieval system,
transmitted or otherwise be copied for public or private use, other than
for 'fair use' as brief quotations embodied in articles and reviews, without
prior written permission of the publisher.

A catalogue record for this book is available from the British Library.

ISBN 978-1-84850-010-5

Printed and bound in Great Britain by
TJ International, Padstow, Cornwall

FSC
Mixed Sources
Product group from well-managed
forests and other controlled sources
Cert no. SGS-COC-2482
www.fsc.org
© 1996 Forest Stewardship Council

Dedication

This book is dedicated to all the wonderful children in my life: Hannah, Callum and Laura, my inspiration for pretty much everything; Chris, a delightful daddy but a child at heart; and my godchildren, Ben, Tilly and William.

Contents

Acknowledgements

First I must acknowledge and thank my own magnificent mum and dad who are always there for me in my most manic moments! My thanks also go to Nik Plevan and Adrian Banger for their input and support on behavioural styles, particularly Nik for his permission to use the animal styles. Thanks to Clare, Debbie and Louise for their help – and, of course, all at Hay House.

Foreword

Dear Allison,

Has anyone ever said to you that being a parent is a bit like riding a roller-coaster? When I got on I thought it would be fun, but being a mum is driving me mad! As I sit here with my glass of wine and bag of crisps, feeling a bit sick and frazzled, I now realize that whatever the ride throws at me, I can't get off and I'm not sure what to do to make it more enjoyable. Obviously there are highs as well as lows. Sometimes I find myself screaming with delight, but most of the time I'm white-knuckled as I hang on for dear life.

Take today. I asked my son to turn off the TV and tidy away his PlayStation games. Not much to ask. This simple request turned into a full-scale battle and now neither of us is talking to each other. I wouldn't mind but this kind of showdown happens on a regular basis. As I torrent through the ride of motherhood at a rate of knots, I sometimes wonder why I got on in the first place. Well, of course the amazing highs make up for the lows, but I want more highs. The out-of-control feeling that accompanies the loop-the-loop leaves me feeling a bit out of sorts. Is there anything you can suggest to help?

Yours hopefully,

Manic Mum

Dear Manic Mum,

People often ask me this question, so I've written **The Manic Mum's Guide to Magnificent Parenting** to give you some answers. It's for you and mums everywhere, who have perhaps become a little manic and want to be magnificent again. It's for all of you who experience the usual day-to-day frustrations of being a mum. It's not prescriptive, but offers ideas based on the principles of effective communication. I've found time and time again that they work. Start using these principles and you'll find that things really will improve. It's easy to follow. I've put them together for you in a step-by-step model called the Seven-step Spiral of Parenting Success. Each week you just study a new step. If you implement the wisdom of the Success Spiral it will make you magnetic to your family. Try it for the next seven weeks and let me know how you get on.

Best wishes,

Allison

Week One:
Goals

Magnetic Principle
Number One

Act like the parent
you want to
become

Welcome to the Madness of Motherhood

Apparently, banging your head against a brick wall burns 450 calories an hour. Why most mothers aren't stick-thin, I'll just never know. When I traded in my Prada for a pram bag, my Polo for a people-carrier and my name for 'Mum', I had no idea what I was letting myself in for. Well, it looked so easy, didn't it? As an innocent bystander, spotting other people's parental *faux pas* was a simple and amusing sport – I'd easily have picked up an Olympic Gold.

With a self-assured smugness, I told myself that things would be very different when *I* had children. With me at the helm of a family ship, surely there'd be no bickering, biting or backchat, no tantrums, tempers or telling-off. I'd have my family whipped into shape like a sweet 99 cone with Flake and strawberry sauce on top.

Whoops, Mr Whippy, did I speak too soon? How wrong can you be? As I morphed from me to mummy, my ice-cream dream slowly melted. I was left standing with only a soggy cone (and saggy boobs), and I realized it wasn't quite as easy at it had first appeared.

Parent or Parrot – What Are You?

What about you? Did motherhood transform you from a relatively normal person into a curious hybrid creature? Did you become an unusual cross between a howling banshee and a parrot on speed? When I had children I didn't realize that in actual fact I'd transformed into a Mynah bird. Like a worn-out 12-inch disco re-mix on repeat, I'd say the same things again and again, eventually losing my voice, the will to live, or some days both. I've often said if I'm reincarnated it'll be as a Macau, with only three piercing phrases: 'Turn it off,' 'Put your shoes on,' and 'We're going to be late.' As you pre-natally dreamed of pink bootees and immaculate children, I bet you had no idea of the impending personal transformation ahead, did you? Now of course I'm not insinuating in any way, shape or form that we don't love our offspring. I'm sure most of us would put our lives on the line for our nearest and dearest, but here's the but – and don't feel guilty, just be honest. Do you sometimes find yourself frazzled and fed up with your family? Answer truthfully, I promise I'm not going to ring Child Line, but, like the man from Del Monte, I bet you just said, 'Yes.'

From the Mouths of Mums

Under normal circumstances I consider myself to be a very nice person, but I tell you what, my kids seem to push buttons that I didn't know I had before, and I feel really bad when I get frustrated and annoyed with them because I'm not normally like that.

Things That Make You Go Aghhhh!!

Before you spend too long beating yourself over the head with a breadstick, just stop and think for a minute what a difficult job it is to be a mum.

It's a fact, our children will challenge us. For the uninitiated, faint-hearted and those of us who just haven't got a clue what to do, it often seems that our children have been pre-programmed to annoy us. At every stage of their development our angels are predisposed to an array of behaviours that push our buttons and send us into apoplexy. Incessant wailing, toddler tantrums, crayon on the walls, untidy rooms, arguments over homework, sibling squabbles, untalkative teens, missed piano practice, teeth not brushed, shoes not cleaned, bikes left on the drive and coats on the floor. Throw sleep deprivation into the mix and you have an 18-year cocktail of 24/7 chaos.

It's Not Easy Being Perfect

If the sheer pressures of being a mum aren't enough on their own, add the fact that these days we're expected to be nothing short of perfect. One hundred per cent wholewheat, organically-grown parents and children, delivered in recyclable cardboard boxes, are the order of the day. Compared to our mothers, the 21st-century parent has a lot to live up to. For goodness's sake, how easy was it for them? They didn't have to cart us from one activity to another with regular breaks for an organic snack. They didn't have to ensure our comfort and safety in cars the size of a small continent, equipped with boosters, belts and surround-sound entertainment. No, far from it, we were left for days on end to roam the country on Choppers, returning home only for food (usually a Wagon Wheel, bag of Wotsits and gallons of tartrazine). In the Noughties the thought of your child walking anywhere without yourself or six bodyguards is an abomination. As for high-tech toys, well, what can I say? My favourites were a lump of dirt, my three 'special sticks' and Granny's false leg. No PlayStations, PSPs or mobile phones for us. Arguments about what to watch on TV? You're joking – you were lucky if there was anything airing on 1, 2 or 3.

Quite frankly, life was a doddle for our parents. Everything was simple, even discipline. Caning, smacking and good hidings were handed out as part of a staple childhood diet. Five a day was the norm back then, and we're not talking about fruit and veg portions! The smacking, shouting and slapdash attitude they dished out would get our parents locked up today.

> *Tip!* Encourage children to work, save or negotiate for things they want, so they value and care for what they have. It's also a great life skill.

All Change

Now, I want to be clear (or my mother will kill me): I'm not saying our parents did a bad job; that's just how things were back then. We, however, live in a different world with different expectations from both adults and children. It's not just our view of parenting that's different. The nuclear family as we knew it has been blown apart. Single motherhood and divorce are on the rise. Dads are on the demise, and the traditional mother's cry of 'Wait till your father gets home' is likely to raise laughter rather than instant obedience. In a lot of families he isn't likely to be coming home anytime soon. Nearly a quarter of children in Britain live in lone-parent families, more than three times the proportion in 1972. And, bless their cottons, when the dads who do still cling to the ethos of the family unit manage to drag themselves home after a 95-hour day at the office, their wobbly work/life balance and poor diet leave them weak and shaking. They barely have the energy to lift a glass of wine, let alone discipline a wayward child. Being a 21st-century mum is tough.

What's It Like in Your House?

Let's turn the spotlight on *you*. Answer the questions below (we're not sending them off for analysis, so be honest).

	Agree	Partly Agree	Disagree
I sometimes shout at my children and then wish I hadn't.			
I sometimes speak to my children in a way I would never speak to my friends.			

	Agree	Partly Agree	Disagree
I nag and get irritated more than I would like.			
I really would like to laugh more with my children and partner.			
I wish I spent more quality time with my children.			
Sometimes I get frustrated because my children seem like they are from a different planet to me. We don't always see eye to eye.			
I just can't seem to get through to my children.			
I often get to the end of the day and feel so frazzled I wonder why I bothered to get up in the first place.			
My children don't always listen to me.			
My children don't always do what I ask.			
I'd like more co-operation in my family.			
My family do things that drive me mad and, despite my best efforts to stop them, they just keep on doing them day in, day out.			

So, how did you get on? Did it get you cogitating? You might think I'm psychic, because I can hazard a good guess that you probably answered a lot of 'Partly Agrees' or 'Agrees' to these questions. Why am I not surprised? Well, in my experience of speaking to many mums and dads, they consistently report these as the types of problems that they experience on a daily basis. Yes, in the real world, parenting is a tough job – and *nobody teaches us how to do it.*

You Don't Have to Be Mad to Work Here But It Helps

Practically every parent I meet, and there've been a lot, thinks they could be doing a better job. I often ask people 'If you could change just one thing about your parenting, what would it be?' Here are a few of their replies:

'I wish I didn't get so cross with my children.'

'I wish I didn't nag so much.'

or

'I wish I didn't get so irritated and impatient.'

Given the domestic melting-pot we find ourselves in, it's not surprising that sometimes we get impatient, annoyed or nag a little bit. And, of course, it's very easy to blame our kids, our environment and our other halves for our feelings of frustration. I've often found when working with mums and dads that they believe the way they feel – whether it be mad, glad, or otherwise – is down to their children.

From the Mouths of Mums

I find saying the same old things again and again so frustrating. After asking my son to come off the PlayStation for the fifteenth time I finally lost my rag, and who can blame me? I had no choice.

Most of us believe that we're not in control of our emotions. On the roller-coaster of life we're powerless; our children are in control of us. They *drive* us mad! There might be some truth in this. If our children always did what they were told, there'd be no need for us to get mad, would there? But what would it be like if you *did* have control? If it were within your gift to feel calm at all times, whatever life or your children were to throw at you? What would it be like if your children did what you wanted and you didn't feel frazzled? I'm sure you'd agree it'd be magnificent, and you're probably wondering how you'd achieve this particular nirvana. Well, read on and find out.

Magnetic Parenting

I'd like to welcome you to the world of magnetic parenting. In this world, parents aren't frazzled and kids co-operate. It's wonderful. So, how does magnetic parenting work?

I'd like you to imagine for a moment that you and your child are magnets. If you happen to have two magnets handy, you might even want to experience the power of magnetism first-hand. Take the magnets and hold them together. What happens? There are only two things that can happen. Either the magnets will attract and stick together, or they will repel and push apart.

Parents and children are just like magnets: they can attract or they can repel. You'll no doubt have experienced attraction and repulsion yourself. Attraction happens on those wonderful days when everything goes just right. It's as if your children are stuck to you by some magnetic bond. It feels great. Then you'll have days where it all goes horribly wrong. It's as if you and your children are like the two repelling ends of a magnet. The more you try to force you and your children together, the stronger the force is that pushes you apart.

You'll have witnessed these forces more times than you've had hot dinners. To illuminate, let me introduce you to my two friends Manic Martha and Perfect Paula. On a trip with her family to Pizza Express, Perfect Paula's children behave perfectly. Paula is relaxed, they laugh and joke and all get on well. They enjoy each other's company and the trip is a pleasant experience.

When Manic Martha goes to Pizza Express, it's a different story. Her kids run riot, terrorizing the other diners. She screams and shouts at them to sit down, but the more irate Manic Martha becomes, the worse her children behave. Like the repelling ends of the magnets, Martha and her children push against each other. Instead of improving, the situation deteriorates and drives them into a downward spiral. Once they're in this spiral it's difficult to break out. As Martha's youngest pokes his brother in the left eye with a fork, Martha loses it. She spirals out of control and leaves the restaurant with tears in her eyes. The trip leaves a bad taste in everyone's mouth and there's acid indigestion all round.

We all have our Manic Martha and Perfect Paula days. When we have good magnetic days we're forces of attraction. We say the right things, we do the right things, we deal with situations in a great way. When we're like this our children seem to interact with us better, even if we're dealing with negative situations. We have put ourselves in an upward spiral.

As parents we can be forces of attraction or repulsion. I'm sure most of us want to be attractive, magnetic parents. So how do you do it? Well, it's as simple as knowing which two ends of the magnet to hold together. To change from repelling to attracting is as simple as turning one magnet around. So, if you're not getting the attraction you desire, just by making small changes to your behaviour you could get the results that you've been looking for. You only have to move one of the magnets to generate attraction. Only you, not your child, has to change for the relationship to become magnetic.

Up-thrust and Down-thrust

I've discovered that there are seven attracting behaviours that will make you more magnetic. Use them in situations where you feel out of control, and instead of sending you into a downward spin they'll break the cycle and push you into an upward spiral. Instead of feeling mad, you'll feel magnificent. I call these magnetic behaviours the Seven-step Spiral of Parenting Success. Use the behaviours at each step of the cycle and it will propel you to the next level. Ignore these steps at your parenting peril.

Over the next seven weeks, each week you'll learn and practise a new attracting behaviour. The great thing is that you don't need your children to do anything for it to work. Just follow the wisdom of each step and, as you move upwards, you'll find things start to change all on their own, because you have become magnetic. When you change your behaviour you'll be astounded by the effect this will have on the behaviour of those around you.

The Seven-step Success Spiral

Let's have a quick look at each of the seven steps in the success spiral.

STEP ONE – GOALS

It must be borne in mind that the tragedy of life does not lie in not reaching your goal. The tragedy of life lies in having no goal to reach. – Benjamin E Mays

Positive change is unlikely to happen unless you know what you want. Asking yourself how you want things to be is a fundamental step in effecting change. When you know what you want, you've created a goal. Without a goal you're like an archer without a target, you've no bull's eye to hit. If you

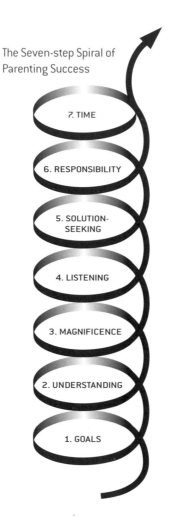

The Seven-step Spiral of Parenting Success

7. TIME

6. RESPONSIBILITY

5. SOLUTION-SEEKING

4. LISTENING

3. MAGNIFICENCE

2. UNDERSTANDING

1. GOALS

don't know what you want from yourself and your children, things will stay as they are.

STEP TWO – UNDERSTANDING

No law or ordinance is mightier than understanding. – Plato

I think sometimes we feel as if we speak a different language to our children, and the meaning of our words and intentions is lost in translation. If you can learn to understand your children and interact with them in a way they appreciate, suddenly a whole world of possibility opens up.

STEP THREE – MAGNIFICENCE

To establish true self-esteem we must concentrate on our successes and forget about the failures and the negatives in our lives. – Denis Waitley

When you start to notice a child's good points, they start to notice them too, and guess what? The child begins to feel great about himself. This feeling of high self-esteem has a positive effect on children's behaviour and the way they interact with you. Seeing magnificence will make you magnetic.

STEP FOUR – LISTENING

The greatest motivational act one person can do for another is to listen. – Henry Moore

With a parent who understands and makes children feel good about themselves, children are much more likely to open up and talk – but do you know how to listen? Poor listening is at the crux of many family communication problems. If you want your children to listen to you, you have to learn how to listen to them.

Tip! Encourage children to feel good about who they are, rather than what they've got. Boost self-esteem by catching them doing things well. Comment on positive characteristics.

STEP FIVE – SOLUTION-SEEKING

Focus 90 per cent of your time on solutions and only 10 per cent of your time on problems. – Anthony J D'Angelo

If you've got children you need the negotiating and problem-solving skills of Kofi Annan. If you can solve problems and family conflicts without war and leave discussions with everyone feeling happy, it'll send you to another level of family contentment.

STEP SIX – RESPONSIBILITY

If people are good only because they fear punishment, and hope for reward, then we are a sorry lot indeed.
– Albert Einstein

People often ask me about how to discipline their children. If you follow the steps in the upward spiral, as if by magic your home will automatically become calmer and your children's behaviour better. If you want to kiss bad behaviour goodbye for ever, I'll show you how to motivate your children into starting new behaviours, and how to discipline them by allowing them to learn from their mistakes so that they become responsible for their own actions.

STEP SEVEN – TIME

Dost thou love life? Then do not squander time, for that is the stuff life is made of. – Benjamin Franklin

Tip! Shower your children with quality time and activities rather than trinkets and designer goods.

Get to Step Seven and you'll have a calm, happy family – utopia. But what's the ultimate, the nirvana, that thing that we're all looking for these days? It's quality time. Get your basics all sorted and suddenly you'll be able to spend more time with your family doing the things that you really want to be doing. Step Seven shows you how to make the most of every minute.

The Downward Spiral in Action

So, how do the seven magnetic principles work in reality? I don't purport to be a paragon of virtue or some expert pontificating from an ivory tower. Believe you me, I've been as repulsive as the next mother and been a participant in my fair share of downward spirals. I've learned a lot of lessons from the Success Spiral, and I've learned them the hard way. The fundamental turning point for me was the recognition that I needed to change my ways if I wanted to be more magnetic. Here's my story of the upward and downward spiral in action.

JUST ANOTHER DAY IN PARADISE
This day was like any other normal Thursday morning. Picture the scene: me in a frenetic furore of toast crumbs, Cheerios and half-eaten Pop Tarts, frantically trying to leave the house, complete with three children, three lunch boxes and a briefcase. Not difficult, you might think, unless of course you've ever tried it – and I'm sure you have! I was tearing round like a crazy woman. The children were being painfully slow – any slower and they'd have ground to a halt. They weren't doing anything I asked, and I'm quite sure that Mother Teresa herself would have been annoyed at a four-year-old complaining that there was a healthy apple in her lunchbox, not chocolate.

'You'll get what you're given,' I told her harshly. 'Think of the starving children and just be grateful for once.'

Yes, this was a normal Thursday morning,

Now, the astute among you will already have noted we're in a downward spiral. Step One of the spiral is *goals*. My only goal was to get out the house. To be fair, it's a valid goal – most of us struggle with this every morning – but at no point did I think about what kind of parent I was being or wanted to be, or what kind of example I was setting. I was showing no understanding (Step Two) of my children's world, expecting them to do everything at the same pace as me, a grown adult. I certainly didn't make my daughter feel magnificent (Step Three) with my unhelpful comments about the apple. I had no intentions of listening to her protests about it (Step Four); I didn't have time (Step Seven) and I wasn't interested. In the magnetic model, I'd committed five acts of repelling parenting and it wasn't even 8.30 in the morning.

Just when I thought nothing else could slow me down, I remembered it was Thursday and Thursday is swimming day. Like a deranged zombie I charged upstairs shouting to my eight-year-old daughter, 'Have you got your swimming costume?' There was no response, so I ran to her room and rummaged through her drawer to find it. In the middle of my flurry, she appeared with a face like thunder. I just ignored it, hoping it'd disappear as I continued my search.

Oh dear, more acts of repulsive parenting. I'd got no time to listen to what might be on her mind (Step Four) and I made no attempt to find a solution to the problem that I could see written all over her face (Step Five).

'Come on, don't just stand there, where's your swimming costume?' I demanded, and before waiting for a reply added, 'For goodness's sake you know it's Thursday, you know it's swimming day, you know we're always running late, why on earth can't you just get your stuff together the night before? Am I the only person who ever does anything round here?' A rhetorical question, not that I was waiting for an answer.

> *Tip!* Give children fair rules and boundaries that are consistently enforced, so they know exactly where they stand and what's acceptable.

Once again I wasn't listening (Step Four). I also blamed her for not having her things ready, when really it was down to me for not teaching her how to be responsible and get them ready herself (Step Six).

The stony stare remained. So I dealt with it the way that any stressed, clapped-out Manic Mum would: I made a completely unhelpful comment.

'For goodness's sake, what on earth is wrong with you? If the wind changes your face'll stick like that. Is that what you want to look like for the rest of your life? Why can't you be a bit more organized? Look at your room, it's such a mess you'd never find anything if you did look.'

Now, that didn't make her feel too magnificent, did it (Step 3)?

The possible side effects of a sudden change in wind patterns seemed to have no influence on her face.

Well, not surprising, really, after so many repetitive acts of repelling parenting. We were in a downward spiral. What I was doing wasn't working. The more I was a negative force, the further down the spiral we went

And then she spoke. 'Mummy, I don't want to go swimming.'

Well, we've all been there, haven't we? Your child doesn't want to do something they're meant to. And, let's face it, it's our job as a parent to make them, isn't it? So I did what any self-respecting parent in that situation would. I turned around and said very firmly, 'It's Thursday, it's swimming day, you're going swimming whether you like it or not.'

Whoops, bad move, we were now about to spiral out of control in a downwards direction. The more I pushed with my repelling parenting, the further away I forced her.

There was a pause for a moment while she processed my response, then she looked me in the eye and said with true conviction, 'Mummy, I hate you!' With that, she turned and walked out of the room, leaving her words to stab me right through the heart.

And here we see the results of repelling parenting. Like two magnets held together at the wrong end, the more I tried to force us together, the more we were pushed apart. I felt like a balloon that'd just been popped. My daughter had told me she hated me. I felt like the worst mother in the world, but I was just trying to do my best. So, faced with this dilemma, what was I to do?

My actions up to that moment had propelled me downwards. I'd made mistakes at every step of the spiral. I hadn't thought about what kind of parent I wanted to be, and certainly wasn't behaving like the one I would have chosen if I'd thought about it (Step One). I was making no attempt to understand my daughter or where she was coming from (Step Two). My jibes about her personality didn't make her feel good (Step Three). I certainly wasn't listening to her (Step Four). My inability to resolve the problem without conflict was clear (Step Five). Although she had no swimming costume ready, whose fault was it that she wasn't organized and responsible? Mine for not teaching her how to be (Step Six). Finally, my lack of time in the morning just escalated the situation even more (Step Seven).

Now, I know that this kind of scenario is a common occurrence in many homes. When we find ourselves in situations like this, we have a choice. We can carry on with our repelling behaviours and keep spiralling downwards until we crash through the floor, or we can change our behaviour and do something different so we become more magnetic. Our inclination often is to stand our ground, exert our authority and insist that our children do things *our* way, but – as I was about to discover – if you want a different result, you have to take a different approach.

Doing something different isn't always easy. As Albert Einstein once said, the definition of madness is doing the same thing again and again and expecting different results. Nagging, shouting or getting angry with people generally leads to defensiveness, denial and annoyance. This inevitably results in a very negative conversation. How many times have you ranted at your children because they don't get ready for school fast enough? How many times has it worked? Let me guess: never? So why do we keep on doing it? As Albert says, we must be mad. Luckily, the spiral tells us what we need to know. Here's how I used it to get a better result.

As I said, doing something different was tricky, because I would have to think what that 'something different' might be. As Step One of the spiral says, I needed to define a positive outcome, or a goal. My goal, of course, was to resolve this situation in an amicable manner. That's Step Five of the spiral. To get there I'd have to understand and listen to her (Step Four) and make sure that I didn't belittle her by talking down as I had been doing. Of course, that would take a bit more time (Step Seven). It would probably make us late for school and I would potentially have to back down from my position of mother in charge. I decided it was worth a try. I took a deep breath and called her back.

She appeared, her eyes filled with tears. I knelt down next to her, put my hands on her shoulders, looked her in the eye and said, 'If you don't want to go swimming, please tell mummy what you do want.'

She looked back and replied, 'I want to stay at school in the classroom while the others go swimming, because I've got some work that I really need to finish. If I stay behind, then I'll have chance to do it.'

'Is there anything else?'

'No, mummy, I just want to finish my work.'

'That's it; you just want to finish your work?'

'Yes.'

'Nothing else?'

'Will you write me a note to say I don't have to go?'

'To be honest, I'm not comfortable with that. I feel like I'd be lying. Do we have any other options here?'

'If you don't want to write me a note, could I just "forget" my swimming kit? That way I can't go swimming and I'll have to stay at school.'

'What will happen if you forget your kit?' I enquired. 'Will you get into trouble, won't you get told off?'

'No, mummy, my teacher never tells anyone off if they forget their swimming stuff.'

'OK, how does this sound? Just for today, you accidental-ly-on-purpose forget your swimming kit?' I winked as I said it. 'You get to do your work, but you will have to live with the consequences if your teacher is cross. How's that?'

'Yes, Mummy.'

'And what about next week, what's going to happen next week?'

'Mummy, I'll go, it's just this week. I need to finish my work.'

'OK, let's make an agreement: you leave your kit this week, you live with the consequences and this will be a one-off.'

No reply was needed. She threw her arms around my neck as she shouted, 'Thank you, Mummy.'

My self-esteem, pride and my sense of being a good mother all returned with that hug. I was filled with a sense of joy. Yes, we would probably be late for school, but I knew that by trying something different and changing my behaviour, the relation-ship I had with my daughter had been strengthened that morn-ing. And all I'd done was take a few moments to do the kind of thing I would have done for any friend or even colleague. I'd set a goal, I'd tried to understand, I'd listened, I hadn't put her down, I'd used collaborative problem-solving. I'd shown her that she'd have to take responsibility for her decision and live with the consequences of her actions, and I'd invested a little bit of time to do this. These acts of magnetic parenting had put us into an upward spiral and got a result we were both happy with. As my daughter correctly predicted, her teacher was unperturbed by the lack of swimming bag and, sure enough, she was able to stay behind and complete her work.

I thought that was the end of the incident, but on Friday when I looked in my briefcase I found a small handmade card. On the front was a picture of a heart surrounded by hundreds of kisses. On the inside was a message which read, 'Mummy, I love you.'

Welcome to Paradise: The Upward Spiral

That incident taught me a fundamental lesson about communication and relationships with my children. The power of attracting behaviours is immense – in fact, it is undoubtedly magnetic. When you get into an upward spiral, it's just amazing the results you achieve, not just in the moment but also in the longer term. I often wonder how many of us spend all our time in downward spirals because we choose repelling behaviours over attracting ones. We force ourselves, our views and our ideas onto our children without engaging them in the transaction. By pushing, we expect them to change and conform to what we want. Although we mean well and have positive intentions, we often end up like a repelling magnet pushing our children away from us.

Tip! Ignore behaviours you don't want. If you're about to capitulate, think to the future: ask yourself, 'What are the long-term consequences for my child of encouraging this?'

From the Mouths of Mums

I know it shouldn't really matter, but every day I ask my children to put their dirty clothes in the washing basket. Where do they put them? Wherever they drop when they fall off their bodies. Who has to pick them up? Me. It drives me mad. I tell them off but it doesn't work.

The Only Person You Can Change Is Yourself

The problem many of us face is we believe we can change and control other people, especially our children. We think we can force them to do what we want. We can make them agree with our way of thinking or our point of view. Anyone who's ever married someone with a view to changing them after the event will no doubt tell you that this is a flawed theory. You can't change or control anyone. As the story about my daughter and me clearly demonstrates, the only person you can change or control is *you*. And if you change, you have the potential to be magnetic. Nobody else has to change, just you. Do this and people begin to react more positively to you. That's the magnetic effect. So, if you're ready to change, read on.

Changing the Habits of a Lifetime?

Deciding that we want to make a change is one thing; actually doing it is often quite another. The main reason many of us find it hard to implement change is that we've fallen into bad habits. Our habits are often so well embedded in our psyche we're not even aware of them or why we have them. Try this quick exercise to get to grips with what I mean.

Exercise

Cross your arms. Notice which arm goes on top, the left or the right. Now cross your arms with the opposite arm on top. Notice how awkward that feels. Now of course it doesn't matter which arm you put on top when you cross your arms, but it's a perfect example of something that you do habitually and probably never think about. If you wanted to change which arm went on top it would probably take a bit of effort until you got used to it.

As parents, we have good habits and we have bad habits. Identifying your own bad habits and deciding what you want to change is one of the biggest favours you can do for yourself and your children, and it's the first step on the success spiral. You are the main influence and role model for your children: they learn to behave by copying you. Behaviour breeds behaviour, so whatever you do, your children will probably do too. Your habits may well become theirs.

From the Mouths of Mums

I remember when my daughter, aged three, stubbed her toe. As she hopped around the kitchen shouting 'Bugger, bugger, bugger,' I knew exactly whom she was copying!

Step One of the Spiral – Goals

So what habits would you like to change if you're to become completely magnetic? The first step in making change is getting clear about what you want to achieve as a parent. And that brings us to Step One of the Spiral: Goals.

If you want to achieve anything, you must have goals. Think about it this way: if you were going on holiday, what would be your first step? Would you get into your car and drive aimlessly round until you found a great vacation hot spot, or would you think about what a great holiday destination might be before you set off? Probably the latter. With a destination in mind you'd know where you were going and you'd make a plan to get you there. If you don't know where you're going, you're like a lost ship at sea, and you stand no chance of getting anywhere anytime soon.

It's almost impossible to change habits unless we know what habits we want to replace them with. We need a goal or target. Without a few clues about what our goals are, our brains get confused and find it really hard to achieve change. Give your brain a goal and it'll help you to make it a reality because it knows what you want. Your grey matter is like a guided missile. Give it a target and it'll seek it out with amazing drive and clarity. If you don't know what you're aiming for, it's unlikely you'll ever find the time or energy to look for it.

As parents, most of us never really give much thought to what our goals are. On the whole we just get on with the job in hand as best we can. At most the goal is to get through the day. Have you ever given any thought to what kind of parent you really want to be, let alone whether you're actually being that parent?

WELCOME TO PARADISE

So, what would it be like if you charted a personal parenting destination and started heading towards it? What if you even arrived there? An interesting thought. What would your goals as a mother be? Just for a moment, think about it.

Exercise

Close your eyes and imagine an ideal family, with you as the parent you'd love to be. Imagine the perfect day, whatever that might be for you. What do you see in your mind's eye when everything is as you want it to be? What's different from now? It might be as simple as getting all your children into the car without a major fuss, or even your youngest eating a sprig of broccoli without incident or complaint. You might see one of those families from an advert where everything and everyone is perfect. Let your imagination run wild.

WHAT'S ON YOUR WISH LIST?

When you've got some ideas, capture them in writing and commit them to paper. Writing your goals down is important. There's lots of research to support the view that penning your goal will significantly increase the chances of you achieving it. Until you capture it on paper, it's just a wish floating aimlessly in your head. You need to transform it into something more concrete and tangible. Most people's goals aren't really goals at all. When I talk to parents I ask them to define their goals. More often than not they come in the form of short statements just like these:

'I wish I didn't get so cross with my children.'

'I wish I didn't nag so much.'

'I wish I didn't get so irritated and impatient.'

These are just *wishes*. To make a goal you need to 'PEP' up your wishes. The letters 'PEP' stand for *positive*, *explicit* and *present*. Your goals need to be written with these three things in mind, and here's how you do it.

Positive Goals

Goals need to be expressed as a positive statement of what you want rather than what you don't want. In a way, it's like shopping. If you have a list of what you want, you're more likely to get it. Imagine going shopping with a list of all the things that you don't want to buy. How difficult would that make it to get everything you wanted? It's the same with your parenting goals. Be positive and clear about what you want, rather than focusing on what you *don't* want.

'I want to be calm and I want my house to be calm.'

vs

'I wish I didn't get so irritated and impatient.'

Explicit Goals

Explicit goals are important because if you're not precise about what you want, your brain doesn't know what it's aiming for. Using the shopping list again, think about what happens when you're explicit and when you're not. The more information you have on your list, the more likely you are to buy the right items. Have you ever sent your other half shopping and he's returned with the wrong food? 'How hard can it be to buy tuna?' you ask yourself. But did you supply enough information to make it easy to achieve the tuna-buying goal? If you'd given the size of tin, weight, whether it's in water or brine and the preferred brand, he'd have been more likely to purchase the correct item. If he came home with fresh tuna and you wanted tinned, can you really blame him for not achieving your goal? OK, I know that you will, but it's not really his fault if you weren't explicit.

Think about how explicit you are in the things you wish for. 'I wish I didn't nag so much' isn't positive and neither is it explicit. It's an expression of what you don't want and it's very vague. To help with this, think about explicit evidence that you can look for that will let you know you've achieved your goal.

For example, write down:

'When I've achieved my goal:

'I will be seeing …

'I will be hearing …

'I will be feeling …

'The date is …

'From today onwards, I am calm. I see happy smiling children who are always pleased to see me and know that I am always calm. I hear laughter many times a day and I'm feeling calm inside. My head feels uncluttered.'

vs

'I wish I didn't nag so much.'

Present Goals

Writing a goal in the present tense, as if you've already achieved it, is a wonderful way of spurring your brain into action. If you write something as if you're already doing it, it's more likely to happen.

Saying, 'I am a patient parent' is much more empowering than saying 'I will be a patient parent.'

There's much more onus on you to become that person if you've already committed to being it.

'I am a patient parent and I listen to my children.'

vs

'I will be a patient parent and I will listen to my children … in three years' time if the wind is blowing in the right direction and I get my act together.'

A Motherhood Goal

If you're not convinced of the power of writing your parenting goals down, just read the goal overleaf and wonder how that might spur you into action if you were to read it every day.

'I am an amazing mother. I always have time for my children and I'm available when they need me. We hear much laughter in our house and I see happy, well-behaved children. I have all the energy I need. I feel happy inside because I know I am doing my best. I forgive myself when I get it wrong; I'm human, after all. My children have high self-esteem and I see their confidence is boosted by what I do with them. They are developing all the skills they need as they grow up. I am developing a strong bond with them that will last a lifetime. Each day I look back on what we've done and I reflect on all the good things.'

ACT LIKE YOU ARE

A goal like this is empowering, and defining one for yourself will put you onto the first step of the spiral. It gives you a clear picture in your mind of what you want to become. Why wait? Why not start to become this person immediately? Imagine what it would be like if you started today and carried on for the rest of your life.

Ask yourself 'What would it be like if I lived the rest of my life like this? What would my relationship be with my children when they are my age and I'm a grandmother or great-grandmother?'

Take a moment to answer the question in your mind. What you do from today onwards will shape the final answer to this question. Your task this week is to create your own parenting goal. The next six chapters will show you some great ways to make your goal a reality, but for this week your challenge is simply to act like you already are the parent you want to be. Gandhi once said: 'We must become the change we want to see.'

HOW TO ACT LIKE YOU ARE WHEN YOU DON'T FEEL LIKE IT

Now, I know as well as any mother that acting like the perfect parent isn't always easy. If you need to find a quick and easy way of stopping yourself from acting in a repelling way, try this technique. It's very effective for distracting yourself and reminding you to act in a more magnetic way. Find an elastic band or bracelet. Put the band on your wrist each morning. When negative behaviour or a bad habit manifests itself, flick your elastic band. This will distract you. Say to yourself: 'I choose not to do that any more, I choose magnetic behaviours and instead I choose to act like ...'

This takes your attention away from the repelling behaviour, leaving you free to choose more magnetic behaviour instead.

Begin to act the part of the person you would like to become. Take action on your behaviour. Too many people want to feel, then take action. This never works. – John Maxwell

Take a leaf out of your children's book. They can make-believe and pretend to be anything they like; why not you? When faced with a situation this week that causes you to want to react in way you'd rather not, behave as if you are the parent you want to be. Ask yourself what you think they would do in that situation, then do it. Notice what different results you get. Be the change you want to see in the world and you'll get the change you want to see. Change the habits of a lifetime: do something different this week and keep your goals uppermost in your mind.

Having a goal and acting like you've already achieved it is the first step on the spiral. Next week we'll step onto rung two of the parenting spiral, and you'll understand where your children are coming from and how to deal with them effectively.

Summary

✫ If you find that your children drive you mad, by changing your behaviour you will affect *their* behaviour.

✫ It's possible to become more magnetic to others by using the behaviours on the Parenting Success Spiral.

✫ The seven behaviours on the Success Spiral are: setting positive goals, striving to understand, seeing the magnificence in yourself and your children, listening, being solutions-focused, encouraging responsibility, and spending time with your children.

✫ If you use these behaviours you will be thrown into an upward spiral. If you don't, you may find yourself hurtling downwards.

✫ Although these seven behaviours may seem obvious, we often don't use them because we've developed bad habits.

✫ The first step in developing new habits is to identify what your goals are.

✫ Goals are the first step on the spiral. They should be positive, explicit and written in the present tense.

✫ When you act like you have already achieved your goals, you will begin to become the parent you want to be.

Week One Actions

Write down the goals you have as a parent. 'PEP' them up: make them Positive, Explicit and in the Present tense. For the rest of this week, act like you've already achieved your goal and you already are the parent you want to be.

Week Two:
Understanding

Magnetic Principle Number Two

Tolerance and co-operation grow from understanding

Have you ever come across that best-selling tome, *Men Are from Mars, Women Are from Venus*? It's a chapter-and-verse description of the differences between men and women, and what to do about getting on with each other. To be perfectly honest, it was no surprise to me to learn that my husband came from a different planet, I'd just never realized it was Mars. After years of picking up dirty pants and objecting to *Top Gear* and endless sports matches on Sky, I knew that our hard wiring was different. Come on, I think most of us instinctively knew that men and women were fundamentally not the same.

So, if men are from a different planet, then where do our kids come from? Well, they're from Planet Kid, of course. And, despite the fact that we must know our children are fundamentally different from us and from each other, I cannot tell you the number of times I've heard a mother cry, 'I can't understand it, I've got three children, I've brought them all up exactly the same, why are they different?'

From the Mouths of Mums

I have two very different children. One is a diligent, quiet boy, he's really no trouble at all. My daughter, on the other hand, is as boisterous and as loud as they come. She's always disturbing my son, especially when he's playing quietly. I'm often frustrated by the behaviour of my daughter and wonder why she's so different from her brother. I sometimes even feel guilty because I'm drawn towards the quieter child, I feel as if I have more in common with him. I wish I knew how to deal with my boisterous girl and feel more connected to her.

The Wonder of Difference

Now, I know we live in a world of standardization and mass production, but we haven't quite got to the point where you buy uniform babies from the deep freeze in Tesco. One day perhaps it will be possible to order identical children who behave perfectly. Children who tidy their room and don't need to have the PlayStation surgically removed from their fingers in order to hold their knife and fork. But until then, I don't think you should be that surprised when you discover that those miracles of nature, your children, are distinctly different from you, and distinctly different from each other. Yes, it's quite normal that one will be like chalk and the other cheese. As they progress through the stages of childhood, they will behave in different and astounding ways that will turn your brain and drive you bonkers. As toddlers they will stomp and as teens they will strop. Yes, mothers of the world, this is the wonder of difference and this is the wonder of being human. Our job is to make sense of it all, and turn them into fabulous human beings while retaining our own sanity. 'Oh, that'll be easy, then,' I hear you cry.

Planet Kid – It's Life, Jim, But Not As You Know It

Because our children are different from us, the first step towards improving understanding is to meet them on their planet and start speaking their language. When you learn to interact and speak to them in a way that they can comprehend, life suddenly becomes easier. They will, I promise, stop driving you so mad.

Often in life the main barriers to communication and understanding are language and culture. If you think about it, 'Hello,' 'Hola' and 'Bonjour' all mean the same thing. Unfortunately, they only make sense to someone who understands the language in which they are spoken.

Just imagine for a moment that you're going to visit a new and exciting country for a holiday. You've packed your toothbrush, some clean knickers and a bag of boiled sweets. You're off, full of excitement, only to find when you get off the plane and into a taxi that the driver can't understand a word you're saying. After ten minutes of rather animated and loud conversation you give up and get on the next plane home. How useful would it be if you could simply speak the driver's lingo?

The same is true with children. How many times have you had those repelling conversations that send you into a downward spiral and leave you wishing that you'd never bothered in the first place? If it's more times than you care to remember, then learning to understand your children might just be the magic pill you need to swallow to rid your family of over-animated, over-heated conversations and misunderstandings.

Learn a new lingo and you have the key that opens the door to understanding. When you open the door to understanding, you take a step up the Parenting Spiral of Success. You become more magnetic to your children. Yes, you will start making sense to them, and they to you. What you're going to learn in this chapter will even help you to understand your other half. OK, I'll wait now while you pick yourself up off the floor.

My Kids Don't Understand Me

Before we get into the wonderful techniques that'll give you these insights into why your children behave as they do and what you can do about it, let's have a little peek at how much understanding there is in your household right now. Think about the statements overleaf to get a handle on your interplanetary communication.

	Agree	Partly Agree	Disagree
I sometimes find that I don't understand why my child behaves in a particular way.			
My child often seems to want to do the opposite of what I want him to do.			
I wish I could understand why my children do the things they do.			
I wish I had ways of dealing with my children that worked.			
I find I get frustrated with my children because they don't want to do things the same way that I do.			
I don't really get my children; I'm not sure where they are coming from.			
I sometimes seem drawn to one child more than another because they seem more like me.			
My children seem to like children who are similar to them.			
My children seem to change the way they behave at different ages.			

I often find myself repeating the same instructions and getting no response.			

If you answered mostly 'Agree' to these questions, or even 'Partly Agree', then you might be wondering why this is. If you struggle to comprehend why your child does things in a certain way, what follows will be a revelation. If you've never understood why your children seem to love mess everywhere, or why they do things more slowly than you, or perhaps why they always seem so challenging, you're about to find out the answers. You're also about to get some strategies to deal with these frustrations. If you want to create harmony in your family universe, you really don't need to realign the planets. There's a much simpler way to do it.

The Power of Understanding

To promote understanding and harmony, all you need to do is start seeing things from your children's point of view. If you've ever seen the film *Freaky Friday*, you'll know it's a great example of what can happen when you begin to see the world from the perspective of your child, rather than your own. In this movie, Jamie Lee Curtis plays a harassed mother with a teenage daughter. By a freakish happening in a Chinese restaurant, she opens a fortune cookie which predicts that mother and daughter will live in the other's body until they understand each other better. After a series of unfortunate and comic events, they are eventually returned to their own bodies after having lived in each other's skin. This experience gives them another perspective. It gives them the opportunity

Tip! Pay lots of attention to good behaviour.

to see the world from the other's point of view, which leads to a depth of understanding and empathy for each other's position, which they never had before.

Being able to see things from your child's perspective creates an understanding which allows you to have a better relationship with him or her.

Think about this in the context of your own life. Have you ever noticed that some people seem to be able to get you to do anything, you willingly co-operate with them? They click with you, they push the right buttons, they seem to be on your wavelength and know where you're coming from. Others, well, they drive you bonkers and quite frankly you go out of your way not to interact with them unless you have to. The difference between the two will usually be that one probably understands you, whereas the other doesn't. We all like to feel understood. When we do, we're generally more co-operative and much happier. Your children are the same.

Unfortunately (or maybe fortunately) we don't have a magic fortune cookie to transport us into the body of our child. Instead, I'd like to share with you a method that I've found very effective for helping parents to get into the skin of their children. It's called behavioural profiling.

Behavioural Profiling

Behavioural profiling is a method I use for helping parents truly understand their children. The origins of this method date back thousands of years. In essence, the notion of behavioural profiling is broadly this: people can be categorized by how they behave. As long ago as 460BC, Hippocrates suggested that people could be categorized into one of four behavioural types: sanguine, melancholic, choleric and phlegmatic.

Over the years, more philosophers and psychologists have concurred with this view and concluded that humans can be broadly split into four different behavioural types. In the 1920s, the eminent psychologist Carl Jung further substantiated this view. He suggested that there are four psychological types of behaviour. He called them thinking, feeling, sensation and intuition. His work forms the backbone of many of the psychological profiling tools that exist today.

So what does this have to do with our children? Well, knowing your behavioural type will help you to understand yourself and your child better. Each of the four behavioural types has distinct characteristics associated with it. You'll probably already be aware that these differences exist, but may never have thought about it in the way I'm about to describe. You'll have noticed that people behave in different ways. For example, some people are outgoing, some are more reflective; some do things quickly, some do things slowly. Just like a recipe for a great dish will consist of different ingredients, we too are made up of varying amounts of four key ingredients. These ingredients make up what is known as our behavioural profile – some people might even say our personality.

Knowing what your behavioural profile is can be very enlightening and give you lots of insights into what it might be like to have you as a parent. It also goes a long way to helping us deal with our children. Knowing someone's behavioural profile is like learning a new language overnight: suddenly you understand what makes other people tick, and a lot less gets lost in translation. You can get to grips with why they act and behave as they do. You're then in the perfect position to think about what you can do to interact better with them to produce more magnetic, less maddening, relationships.

> *Tip!* Set a positive intent for each day. Plan to do one great thing with your children every day.

It's a Jungle Out There

Because sometimes raising a family is a bit like being in a jungle, or even a zoo, I like to think of the four types that make up a behavioural profile for parents and children as four animals. The animals are: Lions, Monkeys, Elephants and Owls. Each of the animals or behavioural styles has its own distinctive characteristics.

☆ Lions tend to be dominant and bold.
☆ Monkeys tend to be full of fun and talkative.
☆ Elephants tend to be steady and loyal.
☆ Owls tend to be compliant and analytical.

All of us, and our children, too, have varying amounts of Lion, Monkey, Elephant and Owl in our make-up. How much we have of each animal will help to determine our behavioural style, or the way that we operate in the world. Yes, just imagine your house is like a jungle, with you as the ranger attempting to keep all the beasts under control. (If you've ever been in my house at teatime, it's not a difficult image to conjure.)

Now the reality is, of course, that we're not animals, but sometimes we take on the characteristics associated with them. To give you more of an insight I'm going to describe the key attributes of each animal. As you read, see if you recognize any traits that remind you of yourself, or of your children. Before you do, though, there's one caveat. Remember that there are as many personalities as there are men, women and children in the world. Although I describe four types, each of us is unique and, importantly, there is no right or wrong type to be. Like a fingerprint, each of us has our own unique profile and, like a fingerprint, it is what it is, there's no perfect one to have.

Bring Out the Beast in You

Lion Characteristics		
Driving	Daring	Confrontational
Demanding	Direct	Bold
Decisive	Persistent	Fast-paced
Aggressive	Problem-solving	Outgoing
Pioneering	Results-orientated	Task-orientated
Competitive	Self-starters	

The Lion Parent

The Lion parent likes to be in charge of their pride. They take a no-nonsense approach to family life and can be quite authoritative. They are competitive and like to win, so might be prone to arguing about trivial things just to be right. Does it really mater what colour beaker your child drinks his milk from, and is it appropriate to have defeated your five-year-old at chess? On the upside, children do know where they stand with a Lion. There's no messing, and Lions are usually good at managing boundaries and implementing consequences.

From the Mouths of Lion Mums

I like to run a tight ship. I wouldn't say that children should be seen and not heard, but I hate parents who can't control their kids. Children need to know who's in charge and do what they're told. They might not like it, but they'll thank me for it when they're older. I know I'm right.

Monkey Characteristics		
Charming	Popular	Cluttered
Inspiring	Sociable	Procrastinating
Enthusiastic	Trusting	Fast-paced
Optimistic	Creative	Outgoing
Persuasive	'Big picture'	People-orientated
Confident		

The Monkey Parent

The Monkey parent loves to be liked. They tend to be great fun, but slightly disorganized. As a result they aren't always brilliant at setting boundaries or making rules. They worry about dishing out punishments for fear of making themselves unpopular. Also, a lack of structure and routine can be the pitfall of a Monkey. Their disorganization means they are usually behind with everything, and their overly trusting nature can lead them to be duped by their offspring. They'll believe piano practice has taken place and homework has been done when really it hasn't. It has to be said, though: a Monkey's child will undoubtedly have the best birthday parties in the land.

From the Mouths of Monkey Mums

I think as a family we have loads of fun. We're always on the go. But I tell you what, we're always in a rush. My kids are always the last through the school gates, and we've usually forgotten something crucial. But hey, you only live once.

Elephant Characteristics		
Reliable	Good listeners	Understanding
Systematic	Patient	Loyal
Methodical	Relaxed	Compassionate
Deliberate	Sincere	Slow-paced
Habitual	Stable	Reflective
Amiable	Steady	People-orientated
Friendly	Team players	

The Elephant Parent

Elephant parents want their herd to be happy and they are big into family harmony. They are very loving, reliable and can't wait to help others. They will really put themselves out for their children. They have a tendency to rescue their children rather than letting them learn from their mistakes. Because they are not keen on rocking the boat, they can be viewed as a bit of a pushover by their youngsters. Like Monkeys, they too can be soft targets. It's easy to take advantage of their kind nature. They like routine and aren't big into change. They're great lovers of the Status Quo (and we're not talking about the rock band). The family holiday is likely to take them to that same place they know and love. They've been there so many times it's got a wonderful familiarity about it. You'll often find that Elephants work in the caring professions such as nursing. They do like appreciation, but if they don't get it they tend to let that fester inside, as they prefer not to share their more negative emotions or worries with others.

From the Mouths of
Elephant Mums

I love being a Mum, it's just the ultimate caring role you can have. I'd do anything for my kids, even if I have to make personal sacrifices myself. I think sometimes they take me for granted and I probably do too much for them, but I wouldn't say anything. I don't want to upset anyone.

Owl Characteristics		
Compliant	Thoughtful	Observant
Painstaking	Analytical	Accurate
Detailed	Precise	Logical
Meticulous	Reserved	Slow-paced
Quality-conscious	Disciplined	Reflective
Conscientious	Controlled	Task-orientated
Perfectionist		

The Owl Parent

Owl parents can come across as quite strict. Everything has to be just so, and they have very high standards that can be hard for children to live up to. They are very keen on rules, and are good at providing boundaries. They will make a child feel secure because of the structure they bring to the family. They often expect perfection from themselves and their children. They'll take their time to make decisions (be sure to give them plenty of notice if you invite their child round to tea). Owls are the most careful drivers and their children have the biggest, safest child seats with extra head buffers.

I have to say I like things to be just right. I think children need rules. In fact, I feel quite uncomfortable if I don't know what I'm doing. If we've got homework to do or a picnic to prepare, we make sure we plan it and get it done in plenty of time. None of this last-minute messing around for me. I read letters that come home from school very thoroughly and, to be honest, can't understand these mothers who always seem to be in a rush. Less haste, more speed, that's what I say.

What Kind of Animal Are You?

As you were reading these descriptions you may have recognized yourself. Yes, in the jungle of life we all have our own styles of behaviour. As you read through the attributes of each animal, you probably identified strongly with at least one of them. Now it's fair to say that we're a mix of each type, but usually we'll have a stronger affinity to one. I for example am a Monkey, but have a splash of Elephant and some Lion, too. I'm not very Owl-like at all.

When you begin to think about the mix of your family in these terms, it's easy to see how things might go wrong. Quite frankly, Lions – with their bold, competitive streak – could eat an Elephant for breakfast, and Owls – with their love of order and need for perfection – could drive a scatty, carefree Monkey to distraction. When you put the whole family into the mix, it really can get quite complicated. The opportunities for sibling rivalry and family feuds, as each animal acts out to type, are endless. This is why learning to walk, talk and speak to the animals you live with in a way they can understand is essential.

Knowing about Lions, Monkeys, Elephants and Owls has been a revelation for me. Within two minutes of finding out about this I suddenly realized why my teenage daughter and I are always at loggerheads. I'm a perfectionist Owl and she's a haphazard Monkey. It's taught me to be less stringent with her, and I'm now helping her learn how to be more organized, not just expecting it to happen by itself. I realized that by adapting to her style we'd get on much better.

Become Dr Doolittle

The summary table on page 48 might help you to decide what parental animal you think you are. As you look, remember that you will be a mix of all four. It's very rare to be only one, and this is designed just to give you a bit of an insight. A couple of pointers to help you. If you're a Lion you probably knew straight away, and you're probably happy to be a Lion because your competitive streak tells you that they're the best! If you're still thinking and want more information before you could possibly make a decision, you're possibly an Owl. If all the other animals look boring to you, then you're probably a Monkey, and if you're drawn to the Elephants because they give you a warm, fuzzy feeling inside and they look like the only kind and caring breed, then that's what you probably are!

> Tip! Thank your children when they do things for you. Acknowledge their contribution so they know you appreciate them.

From the Mouths of Mums

As an Owl I recognize that I can be a bit demanding and possibly not great at giving positive feedback. I'm more task-orientated than people-orientated. So I decided to sit down with my children once a week and have a chat about all the good things they've done over the past seven days. It does seem to work. It's especially good for my Elephant child, who now gets regular positive attention every week.

Now, whatever animal you've decided you might be, it's by no means set in stone and there is no right or wrong. It's a guide to get you thinking about your parenting style and the impact it might be having on your children. You can probably see that, because of the differences between the animals, there is a lot of potential for misunderstandings and miscommunication.

From the Mouths of Mums

My little boy seems so quiet and reserved. I'd love him to be a bit more outgoing and take part in the school play, but he's just not interested. I'm not sure what to do — why isn't he outgoing like his sister, and what can I do about it?

You'll notice on the style chart that there are similarities and differences across the breeds. Some animals interact better or worse with each other because of their similarities or differences. On the right-hand side, Lions and Monkeys are similar in that they do things quickly, whereas, on the left, the Elephants and Owls are more paced and reflective. Here we can see an obvious area for conflict. We can also see from

Where Do You Live in the Jungle?

Owl

Compliant, painstaking, detailed, meticulous, quality-orientated, conscientious, perfectionist, thoughtful, mature, patient, precise, reserved, disciplined, controlled, observant

Likes: Compliance, accuracy, logic, procedures, security, facts, thinking time

Body language: Restrained

Dress: Neat and correctly attired for the occasion

Pace: Slow

Orientation: Task

Lion

Driving, adventurous, decisive, competitive, aggressive, pioneering, daring, direct, persistent, problem-solving, results-orientated, self-starting, confrontational, bold

Likes: Control, choice, challenge, authority, variety, freedom, prestige

Body language: Authoritative hand gestures

Dress: Functional

Pace: Fast

Orientation: Task

Elephant

Reliable, systematic, methodical, deliberate, habitual, amiable, friendly, good listener, patient, relaxed, sincere, stable, steady, team player, understanding, loyal, compassionate, faithful

Likes: Appreciation, assurance, closure, inclusion, specialization, harmony

Body language: Small gestures

Dress: Casual

Pace: Slow

Orientation: People

Monkey

Magnetic, charming, inspiring, optimistic, persuasive, confident, popular, sociable, trusting, creative, 'big picture', cluttered, procrastinating

Likes: Recognition, acceptance, interaction, fun, approval, status

Body language: Lots of enthusiastic gesticulation

Dress: Showy and flamboyant, lots of jewellery

Pace: Fast

Orientation: People

the chart that Monkeys and Elephants are more people-orientated while Owls and Lions tend to be more focused on tasks than people. Again, these differences give rise to clashes and confrontations, because what makes each animal tick is different.

From the Mouths of Mums

My daughter likes her homework to be just so. She'll spend hours perfecting it. I'm always trying to hurry her and tell her that it doesn't have to be perfect. For a while I thought she must have an obsessive-compulsive disorder. What I realized was that I was inadvertently criticizing her. For her it does have to be perfect because she's an Owl. I'm a Lion and 'good enough' is enough for me.

Often what makes us click with another person is that they are similar to us. So, to some extent, Lions tend to get on with other Lions, Monkeys with Monkeys, Elephants with Elephants and Owls with Owls. Now, that's not to say we don't and can't get on with the other animals in the jungle, but in order to influence them, we sometimes need to adapt our style to suit theirs. Using the analogy of a wolf in sheep's clothing makes this sound like it's got sinister undertones, but in reality that's what you've got to do: you've got to get into the skin of the animal you want to relate to, and behave more like them. Do that and you'll instantly become more magnetic.

If you're a Monkey, this could mean slowing down your pace if you're with an Elephant. If you're an Owl, you might have to drop your standards for a Monkey, and if you're a Lion you might need to tone down the hard-line discipline with an Elephant. You have to adapt your behaviour to suit the person you're interacting with. When you get to this level of understanding, it'll project you into a wonderful upward spiral.

From the Mouths of Mums

When I realized that I was a Lion I also realized that I was probably being a bit harsh and demanding of my three-year-old son. I know boundaries and rules are important, but I think I was perhaps being a bit oppressive in my style. I recognized I needed to let him win some of the time or I'd wear him into the ground.

What Kind of Child Have You Got?

So, with all this in mind, let's turn to our children. Your child will also have his or her own distinct style. Before you categorize your children and give them a label for the rest of their life, though, a few words of warning. Children change as they grow up. As toddlers, children may suddenly become more Lion-like as they assert their authority and test the boundaries you've set. As teenagers they may become more reflective and introspective, less keen to share their feelings with you, so more Elephant-like. Use the profiling models to help you understand where your children are today, but be wary of putting them in this behavioural box for the rest of their lives. Children can and do change as they mature. Use this as a moveable reference point, and recognize that their temperament and prevalent style may appear different as they pass through the different stages of childhood.

The Lion Cub

Have you ever met a child who was really challenging? They always have to be right and seem to push the boundaries to the limit? They like to be in control and seem to have no fear. They will try anything and are quite energetic and competitive. These children have a free spirit and are self-starters, always busy doing something. These are what I call Lion Cubs. Quite often when I work with parents, Lion Cubs are a frustration because they are challenging by nature. Lion Cubs often grow up to be entrepreneurs or leaders. As children they're the ones who constantly push the boundaries and like to be in charge.

Have I Got a Lion Cub?

If I say black, my child will say white. I can't understand why she always has to be right. When we play a game of cards, if she doesn't win, don't we all know about it. Whatever limits I set, she'll push the boundaries, whether it's bedtime, lights out or when she has to do her homework. The good thing is she's got lots of energy and always seems to be busy. When the school did a charity event to see who could raise the most money being entrepreneurial, there was no stopping her: cake stalls, car-washing, dog-walking, she did the lot. Even when nobody seemed that interested, she kept going. I think her friends find her a bit bossy, but she does get things done.

The Baby Monkey

Have you ever met a child who is totally charming, enthusiastic, fun and likes to be the centre of attention? They're very sociable, never clinging to a mother's leg when left at a party. They're unlikely to give you a second glance as you leave them at the school gates on the first day. They probably won't be the tidiest of children, and getting them to clear away could be a bit of a challenge. Usually confident in social situations, they are often popular. They tend to be trusting. They like to focus on the big picture, often forgetting about the details of what they're doing. They get things done quickly and can be quite impulsive.

Have I Got a Baby Monkey?

If I say black, she'll laugh and persuade me that it's white. She's very good at getting her own way just by being a charmer. I shouldn't fall for it, but it's hard not to. When we play a game of cards, she likes to win but you know you'll have fun with her. She'll take centre stage and likes to be the life and soul of the party. She's a bit scatty and the state of her room is a sight to behold. I don't think she purposely pushes the limits on tidiness and homework deadlines, she just genuinely seems disorganized and is very easily distracted if something more interesting comes along. I think procrastination is her middle name. The good thing is, she's got a lot of energy and always seems to be busy. When the school did a charity event to see who could raise the most money being entrepreneurial, there was no stopping her. She had so many ideas I couldn't keep up with them all. Some of them were really creative, like a henna tattoo stall. She had no shortage of people willing to help her.

The Elephant Calf

Have you ever met a child who is concerned about others, the one who looks out for his friends and wants everyone to be happy? They like routine and have an inordinate amount of patience. They are usually friendly and do things at a slow, considered pace – in fact, they don't like to be rushed. They are very much team players and don't go out on a limb like Lion Cubs. They like to be loved, and seek appreciation and assurance. They have a good nature and usually listen well. They're quite sensitive, seek harmony and want everyone to be happy.

Have I Got an Elephant Calf?

If I say black, he'll probably just agree. He's not one to get into a state and argue. As long as everyone's happy, he's happy. When we play a game of cards I know he'll give the others chances and sometimes just let them win to keep them sweet. Like any child, he'll push the boundaries, but secretly I think that he likes routine. He craves it if we're away from home. He likes to know what's happening when. He's quite laid back and, for a child, is a really good listener. There's nothing he likes more than to sit and watch TV, having a cuddle. When the school did a charity event to see who could raise the most money being entrepreneurial, he didn't seem that interested. Sometimes I feel like I'm pushing him, but he needs a kickstart sometimes. I helped him to make and sell some cakes, but he wasn't bothered about doing much more, although he was happy to help his friends, who did a tuck shop. He's brilliant with other children and is always the one who helps solve the playground scuffles. His friends think he's reliable and easy-going.

From the Mouths of Mums

I'm a Lion. I'm quite organized and efficient, but my son is an Elephant and he takes an age to do everything. I wake him up 15 minutes before everyone else. It gives him the time he needs to get himself ready at a leisurely pace.

The Fledgling Owl

Fledgling Owls tend to be very good. They like rules and they like to follow them to the letter. They want everything to be correct, and love procedures which are followed precisely. They like time to think and have a tendency to analyse and think about things, so they understand the details. They tend to be reserved and are more likely to think before they speak. They do things at a slow, considered pace, particularly when it comes to making decisions. They'll want to do their homework on the day it's set, and won't want to hand it in until they're sure it's totally correct. Whatever the teacher says goes!

Have I Got a Fledgling Owl?

If I say black, my child will say, 'Why is it black, Mummy?' We'll then have a long conversation about black and all associated things to do with black. He loves details. When we play a game of cards he's obsessed by the rules and is most upset if anybody breaks them. Whatever limits I set, he tends to stick with them. I know all children will push the boundaries a bit, but he seems to like them and enjoys abiding by them. If I go too fast in the car, he'll tell me I'm breaking the speed limit. If he has homework to do, he'll want to do it immediately and he'll want it to be perfect. He spends quite a lot of time on solitary activities like reading or colouring. When the school did a charity event to see who could raise the most money being entrepreneurial, he spent a long time planning and thinking about what he would do. Every detail had to be considered before he went ahead with his garden-tidying service.

From the Mouths of Mums

As a Monkey I realized that I did things far too quickly for my family, and my lack of structure and poor timekeeping were really bad for family life. By my learning to be a bit more organized and introducing more routine, my Elephant child seems to be happier and I've realized that my Owl daughter needs to be given more time to think things through.

Tip! Learn some jokes and make your children laugh.

Animal magic: the language of co-operation

So the differences are obvious and the implications for parenting are plain. Just knowing how your family members are likely to behave is so helpful in determining how to interact with them. If you had to guess what animals your children are, what would you choose?

Animals	Which of my children are most like these animals?
Lion	
Monkey	
Elephant	
Owl	

What's It Like Sharing Your Cage?

It's not always easy sharing your habitat with different animals. What's it like having you as a parent? When you think about your animal style and your child's style, what are the strengths and what things might you want to do differently?

Five Strengths of My Parenting Style
1.
2.
3.
4.
5.

Five Things I Might Want to Do Differently
1.
2.
3.
4.
5.

I used to let my daughter run rings round me. I'm an Elephant and she's a Lion. I now realize that I'm not doing her any favours by being soft and letting her get away with things. She needs firm boundaries and I have to stick to them. She seems to be more respectful of me since I changed. Even though I'm not always comfortable with the idea of disciplining her, I know I have to.

So it's different strokes for different folks. If you don't want to have your cage rattled, you need to learn to walk and talk with the animals in a way they understand and like. Let me tell you an animal story about a family I know well. This family consists of a Lion dad, a Monkey mum, a Monkey child, an Elephant calf and a fledgling Owl. One year this family went to Disneyland for the first time ever. They were all very excited, but they'd been warned about the long queues for rides. The Monkey mum didn't really think too much about this. 'It won't be that bad,' she optimistically thought. 'Let's just turn up and have fun.' Her Monkey daughter thought the same. She'd left all the packing until the last minute anyway, so didn't really have any time to plan what they'd do before they got there. Her Elephant son was happy to go with the flow. Unfortunately, there was no way that the Lion dad was going to waste any time standing in queues or messing about. He wanted to get organized, and his competitive, practical streak made him determined to beat the queues, no matter what anyone else thought.

He insisted that the whole family get up at the crack of dawn even when they were jet-lagged, so they could be in the park first. Then he made them run from one ride to the next. The Elephant, who liked to do things slowly, hated this and complained as he was dragged along at breakneck speed. The Owl was particularly traumatized when Dad was continually reprimanded by attendants for breaking the rules and running in the park. The two Monkeys couldn't understand why they didn't just wander randomly until they happened upon something they wanted to do. Why plan it all? Isn't spontaneity part of the fun?

This difference in needs and approaches led to conflict. But, using the knowledge of animal styles, Mum was able to come up with a solution. She sent the Lion off on his own. He ran ahead, did 'ride reconnaissance', got fast-track passes and brought them back to his brood. They could then do things at their own pace. This meant that all the animals were able to enjoy doing things their way, and Dad got to do things his way, too. Everyone was happy.

I know this is a simple story, but quite often it's the simple conflicts that escalate and lead to family wars. Understanding the people around you can really help to quash family friction.

Creating Your Magnetic Menagerie

So, how can you best use this knowledge about animal styles to help you understand and interact with your family members? Well, it's all about developing strategies that work for your style and your children's.

From the Mouths of Mums

I'm an Elephant with a Lion. I'm quite keen on tick lists and star charts, but to make this more appealing for my Lion son, I decided to add a bit of competition to it. Simple things like asking him if he could beat the number of stars he got last week really seemed to incentivize him. I also made a certificate that I give to the children in a weekly award ceremony if they do well. My Lion really likes this recognition and element of competition.

Here to help are a few strategies to think about when trying to understand what makes your children tick.

LION CUB

Lion parent with lion cub

Think about letting them win sometimes. Is it really necessary to beat a three-year-old at tennis? Make sure you give your child plenty of choices whenever you can. It might be something that doesn't matter like what colour top they wear, but give them options and involve them in decision making. Just like you, they like to be in control. You'll probably be good at setting boundaries, but give lots of praise when they do something well. Ask for their suggestions on what they want and how they want things to be. As a Lion you know how important it is to have your opinion listened to. Make time to listen to what your Lion Cub has to say.

Monkey parent with lion cub

Have very clear boundaries and limits set out. Don't back away from challenging behaviour, confront it. If lines are crossed, be sure to have well-defined consequences. Try to be consistent in the implementation of boundaries and discipline. Don't worry about not being liked for applying consistent rules. Your Lion Cub will respect you if you lay down boundaries and stick to them. Involve your cub in setting the rules. Don't beat about the bush. Be direct and decisive with feedback.

Elephant parent with lion cub

Set clear boundaries and make sure you enforce them. Don't be tempted to back down just to avoid rocking the boat. It'll cause you problems in the long term if you do. Be direct and don't beat around the bush. Say what's on your mind even though you might not want to. Your child is not a mind-reader and needs direct feedback. Use collaborative skills to involve your Lion Cub in the setting of rules.

Owl parent with lion cub

Give some leeway and allow them to choose. Try not to be too critical. Praise your cub wherever possible. Be aware that your need to think things over may be frustrating for other Lions, who like to do things quickly, so perhaps try to pick up the pace. Let them win sometimes and give them options wherever possible – for example, *'Do you want to go the playground or the swimming pool?'* Let them choose.

BABY MONKEY

Lion parent with baby monkey

Make sure you are very clear about what is expected of your child. You may need to write things down so they know what things they must do and when. Make sure you build in time for fun, and give them plenty of time to speak. They love to talk, so make time to listen to what they have to say. Indulge their creativity.

Monkey parent with baby monkey

Help them to focus on the task in hand and don't let them get away with things just so you remain popular. Your Baby Monkey likes to talk, too! Make sure you allow time to listen. Provide structure and boundaries. Be precise about what they need to do, show them or write down instructions so there's no margin for error. Work hard on introducing procedures, but support them in following through and sticking to them, for example with music practice or tidying their room.

Elephant parent with baby monkey

Encourage routine and teach them how to be more organized. Be prepared to let your hair down and have fun. Encourage their creative streak. Make sure you enforce discipline. Your love of routine will be good for a scatty Baby Monkey, who may need help in this department. Be warned: your good nature and kind streak are a Baby Monkey's greatest weapon; don't let them use their charms to walk all over you.

Owl parent with baby monkey

Be precise in explaining what you want. Don't expect a Monkey to remember, or to have the same high standards as you. Ask questions to get information. Pick up the pace and be prepared to let your hair down and have a little fun. Remember, they might find it hard to cope with too many rigid rules.

ELEPHANT CALF

Lion parent with elephant calf

Avoid conflict and challenge when giving feedback; make it constructive and gentle. Give praise and appreciation willingly. Encourage them to tell you what they are thinking, and listen to them. Give them plenty of time to do things. Don't rush them. Let them finish things that they start.

Monkey parent with elephant calf

Slow down and go at an appropriate pace. Allow a realistic amount of time for doing things. Be reasoned rather than emotional with them. Try to listen more and talk less. Ask questions, but not too many, to get to the bottom of how they are feeling. Don't spring changes on them, and warn them if things are about to change. Show sincere appreciation in your comments. Correct and praise privately, not in public. Allow them time to reflect on things.

Elephant parent with elephant calf

Encourage them to take the odd risk. Ask them questions to find out how they are feeling. You both love security and routine, so avoid the temptation to wrap your child in cotton wool and constantly rescue them if things go wrong. Help them to learn through the consequences of their own actions. Think about how you like to be treated yourself when dealing with your Elephant Calf.

Owl parent with elephant calf

Continue to provide structure. Show genuine appreciation and praise, but be careful not to set your standards too high. Give them enough information if you want them to do something or need them to change. Be warm and appreciative of your child and what he or she does. They might not be willing to come forward with information about how they are feeling; be prepared to help them express their thoughts and worries.

OWL FLEDGLING

Lion parent with owl fledgling

Don't be too critical; they are perfectionists and will probably have done their best anyway. Help them to learn how to take action and turn their detailed plans into reality. Slow things down if necessary; give them time to think about decisions and always give them detailed explanations about why you are doing things. They love details and facts. Don't rush them into making decisions; give them time to think about things.

Monkey parent with owl fledgling

Slow down and do things at a more controlled pace. Give them information and data about what you are doing. Try not to be impulsive and rash. Allow time for them to think about things, particularly new things. Listen carefully to their questions and answer them in a considered way. Give feedback which is very specific in nature (they like details). Don't dish out glib praise. Respect your Fledgling's need for order.

Elephant parent with owl fledgling
Recognize that they may like solitary time alone. Be careful not to mistake this for shyness or being unsociable – they like their own company. When praising them, be specific and never go over the top with flattery. Fledglings prefer specific feedback to glib praise. They will probably enjoy and share your need for order.

Owl parent with owl fledgling
Try not to be too critical and expecting of perfection. Praise using specifics. Remember it's important that you listen to them and don't become defensive if they criticize you. Give your child warm emotional support. Think about how you like to be treated yourself when dealing with your Owl Fledgling.

From the Mouths of Mums

The tick list or star chart seems to be the motivation tool of choice in any parenting book I've read. My children liked it, but as a Monkey parent it just never worked for me. I know this sounds ridiculous but with a million other things going on in my day, I found it very hard to keep on top of it. Most days I'd forget to check if the children had done their jobs. They ended up getting frustrated with me. So I invented the marble jar. We have a large clear jar. Every time the children do a good job, I pop a marble in the jar. When it's full, they get a reward. If they do something bad, I take a marble out. It's great because it allows me to be spontaneous in my praise and it also encourages the children to work as a team because there's only one jar. If they both set the table, they both get a marble, if only one of them does it, then only one marble. They understand the maths. This is great for my independent Lion, who could do with learning how to work with his brother.

I'm an Elephant and I think the naughty step is a cruel and humiliating invention. I could never use it.

I'm a Lion and I think the naughty step is a practical, efficient way to discipline a child.

The way we see the world is different and the way we like to be treated differs from person to person. When you understand your behavioural type and that of your child, it puts you in the wonderful position of being able to adapt to suit whomever you're interacting with. It enables you to change your position so you become more magnetic.

This week, really get into the shoes of your kids. Get curious about how it is for them in their world. What's it like on Planet Kid for your little ones? Also give some real consideration to your behavioural style, and work to change your behaviour so it's more compatible with your child's. If you can't manage that, perhaps when they're doing something that used to drive you mad, take consolation from the fact that you understand why and cut them some slack. Remember, they're just being themselves.

Summary

- ✰ Each man, woman and child is unique and individual.
- ✰ If you can learn to understand the differences between people it promotes tolerance and understanding.
- ✰ Behavioural profiling is a useful way of doing this.
- ✰ There are four key behavioural styles: Lions, Monkeys, Elephants and Owls.

Tip! *Try to go for a whole day without saying 'No' to your children.*
Think of a positive way to rephrase what it is you're saying.

☆ When you understand what works for each style, it gives you some insight into how to adapt your behaviour to communicate and interact better with the others.

☆ When you show understanding and adapt your behaviour so it works for those around you, you become more magnetic and tend to get more co-operation.

Week Two Actions

☆ Decide what parenting style you think you have.

☆ Think about what style your children seem to have.

☆ Write out the strengths and challenges of your style in relation to your child's.

☆ Change three things about the way you behave that will make you more compatible with your child's behavioural style and move you towards the goal you set in Week One.

Week Three:
Don't Get Mad, Get Magnificent

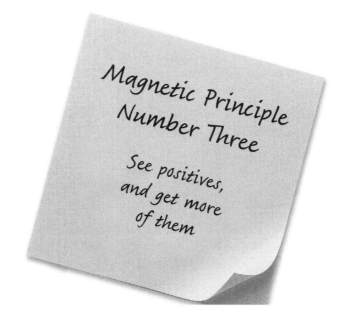

Magnetic Principle
Number Three

See positives,
and get more
of them

So, now that you understand where your children are coming from, this should make it a lot easier to forgive them, to motivate them and to see things from their point of view. It's time to move on to the next step of the spiral. At this point most parents, although happy with their progress to date, are gagging for the hard stuff. They want to know about discipline, how to really whip their kids into shape. What punishments should they dish out to make them toe the line? Now, I hate to disappoint, but discipline as such doesn't come until much later in the book.

'Why?' I hear you cry. 'It's the only reason I bought the book.'

The simple answer is this: I've discovered a way to change you and your family for the better, practically overnight, without the use of retribution or punishment. Those things come later if you really need them, but if you follow the wisdom of this chapter, I'm willing to guarantee that all of a sudden you won't need to be using so many punishments. There will be a happier atmosphere in your home and everyone will feel better about living there, even the teenagers. Hard to believe, I know, but it's true. I promise, if you still need your whip after this chapter, then it won't be for the kids – but let's not go there. That's a whole other book.

The Magnificence Miracle

I'd like to share with you the 'magnificence miracle'. It's a catch-all that will transform you and your family from feisty to fabulous. It's a phenomenon that has the power to make you so magnetic to your children, and to others, that it would be criminal not to tell you what it is and how to make it work for you. So hold your breath no longer, and listen up.

In its simplest form – and anyone who knows me knows I like things simple – it's based on the notion of positivity and the theory that if you make children *feel* good, they're more likely to *be* good. Conversely, if you make them feel bad, then they're more likely to be bad. People who feel good about themselves tend to have higher levels of self-esteem, and there's a clear link between a person's self-esteem and their behaviour. So, if you can make your children feel good about themselves, the theory is that you'll get good behaviour. Your little darlings will be less likely to buckle under peer pressure and will grow into self-assured adults.

Now, let's assume for a minute that this is true. What would it be like if we took that concept one step further? What would it be like if we made our children feel not just good, but magnificent? What would that do for their self-esteem, their behaviour, life prospects – and your general sanity?

The Magnificence Mindset

If this notion excites you as much as it does me, and you fancy getting sky-high on a slice of magnificence pie, then there really is only one prerequisite. There is only one box you have to tick, one contract you have to sign, one rule you have to honour, and it's an easy one at that. The only promise you have to make is to have a magnificence mindset.

'And what,' I hear you ask, 'is a magnificence mindset?' Well, it's all about being open to having a mind that focuses on the positive rather than the negative in life. It's about having an outlook that's optimistic rather than pessimistic.

Let me ask you a question. If I were kind enough to give you a glass of wine filled to the middle, and assuming you were able to keep it from your lips for long enough to notice, would you see it as half full or half empty? Either way you'd be right, but the person who sees it half full has a more magnificent mindset.

Half empty or half full?

The half-empty, half-full debate is one that people will never agree on, and your view on this will really come down to how you see the world. But it's important to note that how you see the world will directly affect how you experience it, and how your children experience you.

Let me give you an example of this mindset in action. When I first learned to ski I couldn't understand why some people seemed to have no fear and really enjoyed it. I was quite nervous, and when I started to ski solo, most of the time I was petrified. As I went down the slopes I told myself I was awful, that I couldn't do it. All the way down I'd be thinking about how difficult skiing was.

After a few times of focusing purely on the negatives, it occurred to me that by doing this I was making the whole skiing experience quite stressful and unpleasant for myself. It took me a while to realize, but finally the penny dropped, that if I wanted to enjoy skiing I had to focus on enjoying it rather than hating it. So I decided to go down the same slopes but with a different mindset. Instead of focusing on what I was doing wrong and what I didn't like, I started focusing on what I was doing right and what I did like. This was a turning point for me. Suddenly it got easier. The slope was the same, but I had changed my outlook from negative to positive. When I did this, instantly the slope was more manageable.

Now, positive thinking or looking for the positive in life might be considered psychobabble by many, but I've seen enough evidence to know that it works. It's true that when you look for magnificence you tend to see it and get more of it in your life. The same is true with bad things: look for them and you'll find them in abundance.

So, on the slippery slope of parenting are you focusing on negatives or positives? Are you contributing to your children's sense of magnificence or are you lowering their self-esteem? Given that those of us with magnificence mindsets live longer, are healthier and happier, why wouldn't you foster magnificence and accentuate the positive? It's just common sense. Isn't it amazing, though, how uncommon 'common sense' sometimes is?

How Do Our Kids Feel?

In a recent study of girls aged between seven and ten, almost all of them made a connection between being physically attractive and being happy. In a world where there are ever-growing pressures on children from advertising, media, peers and school tests, is it any wonder our children sometimes struggle to feel magnificent? For me, the unhealthy images that our children relate to as the norm are epitomized in the recently marketed pole-dancing doll. This effigy to the perfect body, complete with requisite pole, made me feel less than adequate in a number of body parts. So quite what would be happening in a child's mind as they play with it I can't imagine. Is this what we want them to aspire to? Is it any wonder our kids feel less than magnificent, if this is their benchmark?

I think it's fair to say that in our day there weren't so many pressures to conform. There were few designer brands, Bruce Forsythe and Les Dawson were as close as you got to celebrity, and magnificence was measured only by how high you could bounce on your space-hopper. Rapping, ring tones and Reeboks weren't part of the equation. It's easy to see how the 'I'm not good enough' mantra runs through the minds of our children today, as they struggle to match up to the unrealistic images they try to emulate.

This lack of magnificence is also fuelled by a pervading belief that children these days are lazy, lacking and bad. Teenagers are demonized just for wearing hooded tops and caps. In this climate of distrust, it's a case of guilty until proven innocent. But guilty of what? Of being a child? No wonder magnificence is missing. Our challenge is to make our children feel fabulous, so that as they mature into adults, they are able to feel this way for themselves.

Are You a Lean, Mean Magnificence Machine?

Guess what? It's difficult to make someone else feel magnificent if you feel far from magnificent yourself. How you feel and act will, by default, have an impact on your children. Just answer the questions below to get a handle on how magnificent you feel at this moment.

	Agree	Partly Agree	Disagree
People see me as a positive person.			
I expect things to go well.			
I usually see the best in people.			
My inner voice encourages me and tends to be positive.			
If I'm in a group of people who are moaning I will tend to turn the conversation to something more positive.			
When I wake up, I think about all the good things that will happen in the day ahead.			
If things go wrong I can usually see the funny side.			
I feel fabulous about myself right now.			
My children feel fabulous about themselves right now.			
I can list without thinking five positive characteristics about my children.			
In a typical day I laugh a lot.			

On the scale below mark how magnificent you feel on a scale of 1 to 10.

Totally Unmagnificent										Totally Magnificent
0	1	2	3	4	5	6	7	8	9	10

As you think about the way you answered these questions, stop for a moment. If you mostly ticked 'Disagree or 'Partly Agree' with what was being said, think what effect this might be having on your children. Magnificence is magnetic, so the more magnificent you feel, the more positive an effect it will have on your children. It will throw you into an upward spiral. Conversely, negativity is like a bad case of conjunctivitis: it spreads easily, and it's not terribly nice to have to live with. Too much of this and you'll find yourself thrown into a downward spiral.

What score did you give yourself for magnificence, was it 7 or more out of 10? Is there room for improvement? Would you like to score higher? If so, read on.

Manifest Your Magnificence – Or Else

The reality is that if you want to increase the magnificence quotient in your house, then increasing yours will make this task significantly easier. How? Well, when you behave in a magnificent way, your children will, too. But to be a great role model you have to attend to your own needs first. It's a bit like being on an airplane. If the air pressure in the cabin

Tip! Don't expect your children to be able to do what you can. Be prepared to invest time in explaining and training them in new tasks.

drops, a mask will fall from above your head. When placed over your nose and mouth, this mask will supply you with oxygen. The instruction that always comes with the mask is this: 'Before assisting infants and children, fit your own mask first.'

Assuming that you don't see the lack of oxygen as a great opportunity to put a quick end to the seemingly nightmarish experience of flying with a two-year-old on a lap strap, you'd take the advice and attend to your mask *tout de suite*. The general idea being that, until you've sorted yourself out, you're not much use to anybody else – well, not for very long, anyway. The same is true of magnificence. You have to get your own sorted out before you can really help others with theirs. So reach for your oxygen mask, tug it hard and breathe deeply – you're going to inhale some magnificence. It'll make you feel better and fly higher than gas and air.

The Quest for Magnificence

How does magnificence find its way into your body? How do you get it into your being so you live and breathe it? Quite simply, you have to seek it out. It needs to be firmly on your agenda and then, when you find it, you can put it where you want. There's an old saying that goes, 'You get what you focus on.' Personally I've always found this to be true, and I know that many of the parents I work with have found it to be true, too.

You can saddle yourself with a mindset of misery or a mindset of magnificence. The choice, as they say, is yours. If you choose to opt for magnificence, what a difference it will make. So what are you focusing on? You have a choice, like me on the ski slope: you can focus on magnificence or you can focus on negativity. Whatever you choose, you'll get more of it.

What glasses are you wearing?

Finding magnificence in yourself is as easy as wearing a new pair of glasses. Let me explain what I mean. Just look at your surroundings for a moment and notice what you see. Notice the colours and the brightness, the hues and tones of everything around you. When you've taken that in, imagine that you're looking at the same vista through a pair of sunglasses. If you've got a pair handy, you might even want to put them on. Wearing sunglasses makes the scene look different. Chances are things look duller, and darker, the sky less blue and so on. However, although the scene appears different, the reality of the situation has not changed. The sky is still blue, whatever colour glasses you're wearing. If you wore rose-tinted spectacles, everything would have a pink tinge to it. The reality remains exactly the same; what changes is the way you see it.

The same is true with life generally. We filter out certain things. When it comes to our children, for some unfathomable reason we tend to filter out the positives. We more often see what they are doing wrong than what they are doing right.

This is very worrying when you consider that the phenomenon of filtering can be extremely powerful. I once went to see a stage hypnotist, where the volunteer (or victim, I'm not sure which to call him), was given a huge pair of 'Elton Johnesque' spectacles to wear. The hypnotic suggestion was made to him that whenever he put these spectacles on, he had the power to see through people's clothes. While he wore the spectacles, everyone appeared to be completely naked. In his mind this man really did believe that everyone sitting in the Royal Albert Hall was starkers. Apart from being extremely funny, this demonstrated the power of the mind to see what you suggest to it.

Be a magnificent mum in a flying machine

Now, some of you will find the idea of being able to see everyone's nakedness appalling, and some of you will find it appealing. I'm not going to suggest that you try it, particularly if you spend a lot of time around middle-aged mums and dads (not pleasant). I have a much grander and more powerful idea for you to try out this week, and that's focusing on magnificence. I want you to imagine that you are wearing a pair of new designer specs, a fabulous brand called 'Magnificence'. When you put on your 'Magnificence' specs, all you can see is the good in any situation. Nothing negative can get through. When you're wearing these, your wine glass will always be half full. Just like dogs can't see the colour green, bees can't see the colour red, and men never see the pants they've left lying on the bathroom floor, you won't see negatives, only positives.

I know what you're thinking: 'This is absolutely bonkers. How can I possibly get through a week without seeing badness, because, let's face it, that's what my kids do best?' Well, I promise you, give it a try and you'll be amazed by the results.

Every morning for the next week, when you get up I want you to reach for your 'Magnificence' specs and put them on, because this week you'll be filtering out the bad and seeing only the good and great in everything, starting with yourself. Try the Mum's Magnificence Miracle exercises to get you started on your quest for self-appreciation. I'm not saying you'll turn into a new person overnight – they're not really miracles – but having an awareness of how you're behaving and what you think about yourself can be very powerful. And these simple exercises could change the way things work in your home.

Mum's Magnificence Miracle One: Blow Your Own Trumpet

Whenever I work with people, I always ask them to tell me five brilliant things about themselves, five things that make them feel magnificent. Now, of course we're all naturally modest, and don't want to appear boastful, but if you can't identify your own fabulous attributes, how will anyone else? Hide your best bits under a bushel and it's hard to let them shine. So, write down the five most magnificent characteristics about yourself – more if you like. What are you great at? What are your unique qualities? How would your friends describe you, your partner and your children? Are you optimistic, kind, funny, honest, intelligent, happy, energetic, organized, patient, thorough, a good listener? Where do you excel? Ask your children what they like best about you and write it all down.

☆ I am …
☆ I am …
☆ I am …
☆ I am …
☆ I am …

Next, collect a list of all the things you've done that made you feel great. What have you achieved in your life that's significant? What are the things that make you feel good about yourself? Just revisiting these achievements or positive aspects of your life can be very affirming. Again, write them down.

☆ I have …
☆ I have …
☆ I have …
☆ I have …
☆ I have …

Tip! *Avoid using clichés with your children: 'If you don't eat that I'll send it to the starving children' or 'If the wind changes your face will stick like that.' They don't work.*

From the Mouths of Mums

Sometimes when you get stuck in the day-to-day grind of life you forget to step back and think about how much you've achieved and that you are a worthwhile person. By creating my list and looking at it each day, it reminded me that I was more than just a nappy-changer and food-preparation machine!'

Mum's Magnificence Miracle Two: Wear Your Magnificence Specs

With your best attributes identified, the next step is to put on your 'Magnificence' specs. Start using them to spot yourself at your best. Keep your paper with your attributes and uplifting experiences nearby, perhaps in your purse. When you look in the mirror in the morning say to yourself:

'I am … funny' or 'intelligent' or 'patient' or 'loving', or whatever your attributes are. Refer to your list once a day. Remember that you get what you focus on. As you go through your day, notice when you exhibit your best attributes. Seize opportunities to be the unique and brilliant you. If you're a funny person, be funny; if you're a patient person, be patient. Remember to use the 'Act Like' technique from Week One.

One of my favourite garments is my 'boasting T-shirt'. I wrote all my achievements and best attributes on it in a fabric pen, and when I feel less than magnificent I put it on. Wearing it reminds me to demonstrate the attributes that make me who I really am when I'm at my best. It has a great knock-on effect for me and those around me, especially my children.

Mum's Magnificence Miracle Three: Tune Out Miserable, Turn Up Magnificence

I'd like to introduce you to Mira and Mary. They're the two little voices in my head that constantly try to influence me. In fact, I've got several and I'm on first-name terms with them all. Like Ying and Yang, Mira tries to make me feel miserable while Mary tries to make me feel magnificent.

If you've also heard voices, then don't worry, you're not going mad. It's quite normal and most of us do have an inner voice. The interesting thing is what they say to you and how they influence you. Do they make you feel miserable or do they make you feel magnificent? Ever stood in front of the mirror and heard your inner Mira say, 'You look fat today'? If so, how did it make you feel? Ever done a piece of work and, as you finished, heard Mira pipe up, 'That's not good enough'? Your internal voice usually has an opinion on how well or how badly you're doing, and it's not shy about coming forward with opinions.

'You look fat today.'

'Why did you put that on?'

'You shouldn't have said that, you'll look stupid.'

'Don't do that, it won't work.'

'Why do the children always annoy you?'

When you look in the mirror does your inner Mary ever say,

'Wow, you look fabulous today'?

'You are going to have a great day today'?

'The children will really behave today'?

When it comes to your inner voices, you have a choice. Do you want to listen to comments that make you feel miserable, or do you want to hear something more affirming that makes you feel great?

Your challenge is to notice the voice in your head and decide when you will listen to it and when you won't. I want you to encourage it to say things that make you feel magnificent. Listen intently when it does, and turn down the volume when it says things you're not keen on.

How do you turn down the volume? Well, a couple of choices. Either ask it to be quiet, or pretend that you have a volume control knob on the side of your head. Just turn it to the lowest setting. I know it sounds crazy, but give it a go, you might just be surprised. Take control of your inner voices. Turn up the ones that make you feel magnificent. Tune out the ones that make you feel miserable.

Mum's Magnificence Miracle Four: Get Rid of Negative Emotions

Our negative emotions often pull us down and make us feel less than our best. Two of the constant offenders in the world of mums are guilt and worry. Before children I only associated guilt with hardened criminals, convicts and my secret stash of Ferrero Rocher under the bed. But with motherhood came opportunities as endless as Imelda Marcos's shoe collection to experience guilt, and worry, on a grand scale. If you're a victim of these mental pariahs, then you'll know they're as pleasant as piles and as helpful as a chocolate teapot.

What do they do for us? The truth, the whole truth, and nothing but the truth, is that they're worthless emotions. In the mental courtroom of your mind they suck you dry of cerebral energy, making you feel bad as you accuse yourself of heinous crimes:

'Possession of an overflowing ironing basket m'lord, supply of a non-organic apple, getting impatient with the children.'

It's hardly mass murder, but the verdict is always same: 'Guilty as charged.' Your punishment is a life sentence of remorseful wallowing in misery, not magnificence. I say, 'Objection, your honour!' Feel good about yourself and get rid of guilt and worry.

This week, why not channel your time and energy into feeling great instead of guilty? Generally guilt revolves around decisions you made in the past, and however much cross-examination takes place, they can't be changed. Why waste your resources dwelling on them? Instead, choose to be bold and decisive about your decisions and live happily with the consequences. Remember, the only person who has control over how you feel is you. If you can't live with a decision, then make a different choice, one that makes you feel magnificent.

Exercise

To stop guilt and worry in their tracks, try this on for size:

1. Think of something that makes you feel guilty, like nagging the kids or eating too many biscuits. I'm sure you have many of your own!
2. Take responsibility for these actions and your choice to feel guilt or to worry.
3. Decide how you would prefer to feel. Instead of playing chief prosecutor, think of practical actions you can take

to change your situation and emotional state. Perhaps decide to feel calm instead of manic. It is only a sate of mind, and you do have some influence over it.

4. If guilt and worrisome feelings remain, take action. What can you do to get control? Stop nagging, change your routines, buy the organic apples. Do what you have to so you can alter your mental state.

How you feel is, to a large degree, up to you. This week be your own judge and jury. If guilt and worry show up in your courtroom, throw them out for contempt and focus on things that make you feel magnificent.

Mum's Magnificence Miracle Five: Do Things That Make You Feel Magnificent

What makes you feel great? Often we don't feel fabulous because we're not doing things that make us feel magnificent. It's oh so easy as a mum to get sucked into work and domestics, domestics and work. Just stop and think for a moment. When was the last time you did something that made you feel really fabulous or laugh out loud? If it was too long ago, ring the changes this week. Is there something that you could do for yourself that would set you on the road to magnificence? Is there something you've been putting off? Is it a diet, starting a course, catching up with friends, maybe a night out? Write it down. Whatever it is, I guarantee that when you do it, you'll instantly get a buzz and start to feel better.

> One thing I commit to doing this week that will make me feel magnificent:

If it's a big thing and you don't think you can do it all in one go, take a small step towards making it happen. Perhaps building an extension to your house so you have more space for all the kid's stuff would make you feel better. You can't do that in a week, but you can take a small step towards making it happen. Perhaps contact an architect, draw up your ideal layout, anything that takes you in the direction of achieving something that'll make you feel good about yourself. Take one baby step. Select one thing that would make you feel magnificent about your life right now. Put it in your diary and start making it happen.

Eliminate things that make you feel bad

Start to notice what makes you feel negative. Make a mental note of how you feel throughout your day. When you're not feeling fabulous, what is it that's bringing you down? Is it kid's clutter, the clothes you're wearing, boredom with the same old routine? Whatever it is, make a note and take a small step towards eradicating it.

One thing that makes me feel negative:
What will I do to eradicate it:

When you begin to take positive action, you start to feel in control. When you feel in control, you feel better. When you don't feel magnificent, just ask yourself the question 'What's one thing I could do right now to make myself feel better?' Whatever it is, just do it.

Tip! If your children constantly overstep the line, think about how you can support them rather than rescuing them.

You catch more flies with sugar

So, with you feeling magnificent, or certainly better than you did, it's time to tackle those children of yours. How do you raise their standing in the magnificence stakes? Well, just imagine for a moment that I'm standing in front of your little angel and I have a sugar bowl and a salt cellar in my hand. The sugar bowl is full of something deliciously sweet, something that they'd love to get their chops round. The salt cellar, surprise, surprise, is full of salt. My guess is that given the choice between the salt and the sugar, they'd go for the sugar every time.

Children crave sweetness, they crave love, they crave positive strokes. And what happens when we are sweet to our children, when we are positive about and respectful to them? Well, they behave better. When we're nice to them, their self-esteem rises; when we're nasty, it's diminished. Spread a little sugar round the place for your children. My granny often used to say 'You catch more flies with sugar,' and Mary Poppins herself was a great advocate of the white stuff. So from now on, whenever you interact with your children, think about what impact your actions or words are having. Is it positive or negative, magnetic or repelling?

Kids' Magnificence Miracle One: See Their Magnificence Shining Through

We often spend too long preoccupied with our children's bad points, but like the sun through the clouds, make it your mission to see their best attributes shining through each day and I promise they'll start to shine more brightly. With your 'Magnificence' specs perched firmly on your nose, from now on I want you to filter out the negative in your children. Of course, before you can do that you need to know what their positive characteristics are. Just as you did for yourself, ponder for a moment on the wonderful and unique qualities of your children. Now write them down.

Five magnificence characteristics of my child:

1.

2.

3.

4.

5.

Make a point of remarking on these characteristics when you see them in action – obviously not every moment of the day – that would seem false and unnatural – but when you see your child being kind, or helpful, or whatever their best attributes are, notice it and tell them you've noticed.

From the Mouths of Mums

My daughter is exceptionally kind. She loves animals and looks after her rabbit with real compassion and responsibility. With a lot of other things she's a bit absent-minded and often forgets school books and everyday things. I realized that I spent a lot of energy focusing on this, and it occurred to me that I'd not told her how kind she was and how responsible she was with the rabbit. When I started to notice that more often and tell her I'd noticed, it seemed to have a knock-on effect in other areas.

Kids' Magnificence Miracle Two: No More 'NOs'!

Have you ever counted the number of times you say 'No' to your children? I bet it's loads, and if you've ever found it seems to fill them with a devilish determination to do whatever you've told them not to, then I'm not really surprised.

Why? Let me explain. I want you to contemplate what happens when you tell someone they can't do something. Let's demonstrate by using you as a guinea pig. In a moment I'm going to ask you not to think about something. I want you to try as hard as you can *not* to think about this thing. As if your life depended upon it.

Ready? OK, here goes... Whatever you do, *don't* think about having a wild, passionate embrace with Brad Pitt. Whatever you do, you mustn't let thoughts of you and Brad enter your mind. Do not think about having a wild time with a Monsieur Pitt.

Now, let me guess: even though you tried hard not to think about Brad, you probably got a little flash of him in your mind, didn't you? Don't be afraid to admit it, I'd be very surprised if you didn't. I asked you very clearly not to, but I bet you still did. Now, does the fact that you've had thoughts of passion with a stranger mean you're a bad person who should have all treats withdrawn for a week? No, it doesn't, because actually it's not your fault. The reason you probably thought about Brad is that our brains work in a weird and wonderful way. For us *not* to think about something, first of all we have to picture it in our mind, so we understand exactly what it is we're being asked not to do. So, ironically, asking you *not* to think about Brad Pitt is possibly one of the best ways to get you thinking about him.

How does this relate to our children? Simple: by asking them not to do something, we immediately cause them to think about doing that very thing! Conversely, when we start telling our children what we want them to do rather than what we *don't* want, we begin to get better results. By changing the way we phrase things from negative to positive, what flashes up in their brain is a positive image. Here are some examples of what I mean:

'James, don't knock that cup over' (negative) becomes 'James, please be careful with that cup' (positive).

'Don't be so cheeky to your father' (negative) becomes 'Please be polite to your father' (positive).

'Don't touch that hot pan' (negative) becomes 'Please stand over in the corner by the table as the hot pans are dangerous and could burn you' (positive).

'Don't slam the door like that' (negative) becomes 'Please shut the car door gently and look first to make sure there are no fingers in the way' (positive).

'I wish you would stop leaving your dirty underwear on the floor' (negative) becomes 'I would be really grateful if you would put your dirty washing in the basket, or even better by the washing machine; that would really help me out' (positive).

Try to get through this week without using the word 'No'. Obviously, if your inquisitive two-year-old is about to stick the finger he has just licked into an electrical socket, asking him politely and respectfully to go and stick his finger somewhere else may not be the best course of action. In this scenario, feel free to yell 'NO!'

Kids' Magnificence Miracle Three: Label with Care

We live in a world of labels. To make things easy for our brains to understand what's going on and to simplify our lives, we tend to categorize and label everything. When we stand in the supermarket we look for carrots under the label 'vegetables' and milk under the label 'dairy'. Generalizing and categorizing assist us in processing huge amounts of information. A label can also act as a guide or instruction. If a hill is labelled as steep, we know to go down a gear. Labels influence how we behave. Even something as simple as a name, that most fundamental label, can have emotive connotations. I remember when my husband and I were choosing a name for our first child, we asked people for their views. With every name we suggested, somebody seemed to have a negative association. To protect the innocent I won't reveal the names, but the associations ranged from cheeky, naughty and quiet to trouble-maker.

What kind of things do you say about your children, without thinking about what labels you are giving them? In true 'give a dog a bad name' style, when we have a label we tend to live up (or down!) to it. Here are just a few I've heard over the years:

'You're so silly.'

'What a naughty little boy you are.'

'He's so shy.'

'She's a right little madam.'

'You're bone idle.'

What are the consequences of these labels? Well, the truth is, we begin to believe that they're true. We live up to them, and act as if we are that label. In the same way that we respond to our name and not to the name of someone else, we learn to respond to our label.

What life labels are you giving your children?

I once worked with a lady who was amazing at maths. In fact, she was outstanding. As a child she'd always been told how good she was with numbers, and her belief in her maths magnificence had remained with her throughout her life. However, another remark made by a teacher many years earlier had also stayed with her. This unthinking teacher had told her that beauty and brains didn't go together. The result of this insensitivity was a child, and later an adult, who labelled herself as ugly. She knew she was good at maths, but could never believe she was pretty as well. This hindered her in finding a boyfriend and her self-esteem was low.

Another example of the power of labels was demonstrated back in 1968. Jane Elliot conducted a now-famous exercise in response to the assassination of Martin Luther King. To help explain racism, she told the children in her class that all the children with brown eyes were superior to the children with blue eyes. The result? The brown-eyed children behaved in a superior and derogatory way to the blue-eyed children. Their behaviour was influenced by the label they'd been given.

The labels you give your child will directly influence their performance and behaviour. So if you want magnificence, you have to expect and look for it. Imagine that your children wear an invisible badge that says 'I am magnificent.'

Kids' Magnificence Miracle Four: Mind Your Language

Using positive, encouraging language will make your children feel more valued and increase their sense of self-worth. Think about some of the things that you say to your children. Do you use the language of attraction or do you use repelling language? Start to notice when you use generalizations and exaggerations like 'You never try.' Are you ever sarcastic or hurtful with what you say? Take a look at the phrases below to draw inspiration from or to avoid.

Magnetic language

I love you just the way you are.
I love playing with you.
I felt so proud of you when I saw you …
You make me feel so happy.
I love sharing with you.
I really enjoy it when we …
I get so excited just before I see you.
Jinny said how well behaved you were at her house.
I enjoy spending time with you because …
It was great when you …
You are very special to me because …

You put a lot of effort into that.

Would you like to try that on your own? I think you can do it.

Your teacher told me how hard you've been working.

I know you can do this on your own.

You're very good at ...

Repelling language

Exaggeration and Generalization

You never do anything.

You're always late.

I've told you a thousand times.

All you ever do is whine.

Nobody can run fast in this family.

Boys never concentrate like girls.

Unempowering Comments

You'll never be able to do that.

You're just trying to get round me.

You'll have me in an early grave.

Just get out of my sight.

You're acting like a baby, not a three-year-old.

Who do you think you are?

Stop doing ...

I wish you wouldn't ...

Why don't you think before you speak?

We work our fingers to the bone for you.

You're so ungrateful.

You're driving me up the wall.

I don't know why I bother.

Tip! Talk favourably about your children when they are in earshot.

Unhelpful Comparisons

If only you were as good as your brother.
My mother would never have let me get away with that.

The language of magnificence

This week, make an extra-special effort to use the language of magnificence to encourage your children and boost their self-esteem.

Kids' Magnificence Miracle Five: Look for the Silver Lining

Now, I know sometimes it's hard to see the positive in everything. Little Jinni has just crayoned all over your beautiful, newly decorated walls. William comes down with flu-like symptoms just before you're about to go out for dinner. Joe seems unable to progress at maths, he's bottom of his class. These are not scenarios that will necessarily make you jump for joy. So how do you make the best out of a bad job and see magnificence in even the most challenging situations? I'd like to introduce you to a technique that I learned a few years ago. It's called *reframing*.

Reframing really helps to put things into perspective. When bad things happen that you can't change, it allows you to extract something positive. Reframing events can often create new opportunities and allows you to approach situations in a more empowering way. Here are two ways you can use reframing.

Reframe one: look for the opportunities

William comes down with the flu. Instead of a night out ruined, reframe it as:

★   a chance to spend some quality time with William

☆ a chance to have a night in
☆ a chance to save money on the babysitter and dinner, perhaps to treat yourself to something else you've been wanting.

The possibilities are endless!

Reframe two: look at it another way

Joe is at the bottom of the class. Instead of a cause for family sadness, reframe this as:

☆ The only way is onwards and upwards; we like a challenge.
☆ Joe is brilliant at a number of other things; with help his maths will improve too, and we can support him in this.

From the Mouths of Mums

My daughter wet her bed for the third time this week. 'How on earth do you reframe that?' I thought. Well, I guess I'm grateful her electric blanket wasn't on!

Kids' Magnificence Miracle Six: The Joy of Love and Laughter

It's really hard to feel bad about yourself – or about anything else, for that matter – when you're laughing. As they say, laugh and the whole world laughs with you. With a growing body of evidence that laughter makes you live longer, I'd

> *Tip!* Notice what you need in order to be the parent you want to be.

say getting a dose every day has to be a good thing. And the buzz that you'll get from making another human being laugh is totally awesome. Making small children giggle has to be one of the easiest things on the planet, but often we don't do it because we're stressed, fed up, or perhaps it hasn't crossed our mind. Have you ever noticed how an uncle or friend can often make your kids laugh, but you can't? This week, focus on making your family laugh at least once a day. I recently did a course in stand-up comedy, where I learned that pretty much anything can be funny. Children don't have the most sophisticated sense of humour. Blow a few raspberries, do a silly dance, tell a joke, make your kids giggle. The important thing is just to relax and enjoy being with your kids and let the humour come spontaneously.

Having a magnificent mindset is the most wonderful thing. With a positive outlook, life not only seems better, it *is* better. When you feel magnificent you suddenly become more magnetic to others and you'll find yourself in more upward spirals. So next time you start to notice that your kids are driving you mad, don't see red, see magnificence!

Summary

☆ When children feel good about themselves, they behave better.

☆ You can choose to see the world in a positive way or a negative way. Either way you'll get more of what you choose to see.

☆ When you see the positives in children it helps to raise their self-esteem.

☆ When you feel magnificent it has a positive knock-on effect on your children.

☆ You get what you focus on, so focus on positives rather than negatives when dealing with your children.

Week Three Actions

☆ List the unique and magnificent qualities of yourself and your children.

☆ Spend the next week wearing your 'Magnificence' specs and filter for positives.

☆ Do something that makes you feel great.

☆ Avoid the word 'No.'

☆ Phrase things positively.

☆ Use reframing to see the positive, even in situations that might appear negative.

☆ Laugh often.

Week Four:
Listening

Magnetic Principle
Number Four

Listen more,
talk less

It's Like Talking to a Brick Wall

Now you're feeling magnificent and so are your
You're all sweetness and light, and I'm certain tha. you'll
have noticed an improvement in their behaviour and possibly
yours. If you've been using the success spiral strategies on
your other half, you might even have noticed that he's not
driving you quite so mad either. Now it's time to move swiftly
up the spiral and solve the perennial problem faced by many
a mother. Something that from time to time drives us all mad
and sends us spinning down the spiral quicker than you can
say, 'You're not leaving the house looking like that, young
lady.' This, of course, is the issue of lacklustre listening and
chaotic communication. I've found this is an ailment rife in
all families, with men seemingly particularly predisposed to
what I call 'cloth ear' or selective hearing. And, quite frankly,
when you're on the receiving end of a person who seems to
ignore every instruction, sentence or piece of information
you deliver, it's no wonder you ask yourself 50 times a day,
'Does anybody listen to a word I say?' If 'I might as well be
talking to a brick wall,' is a constant refrain in your house,
you're not on your own.

For me, the notion of a mother being driven mad by the
lack of listening in her house is epitomized in the wonderfully
funny film *Shirley Valentine*. In this, the main character is a
wife and mother whose husband and children pay her hardly
any attention. You might remember that throughout the film
Shirley converses with the wall in her kitchen, as it seems
to be the only thing in her life she can be sure won't run off
before she's finished speaking. It makes amusing viewing, but
you know what they say: there's a thin line between comedy and tragedy, and underneath this humorous portrayal
of a worn-out middle-aged housewife we are also shown the
underlying sadness that sends her to Greece where she falls
in love with a toy boy! This might be a slightly drastic action

to take, but I'm sure many parents can relate to Shirley's sentiments of 'Why do I bother? Who listens anyway? I might as well be talking to the wall.'

From the Mouths of Mums

How on earth do you make children listen? Are the only options repetition and shouting? Please tell me that there is another way.

Beyond the Brick Wall

Most of us are quick to denounce others for not listening to us. I know I'm guilty of it. How often have you said to your partner or child, 'You just don't listen to a word I say'? Before you begin counting up what seems an infinite number of occurrences, ask yourself *why* they don't listen. Could it be, perhaps, that despite our best attempts, most of us are atrocious listeners ourselves? Maybe the reason they don't listen to us is that we don't listen to them? Studies show that a lot of what we say to our children is directive. We're like human radios. We transmit information fabulously, but we don't always receive it too well. Like a radio station, if the target audience doesn't like what it's hearing, it tunes out. Who wants to listen to Nag FM all day?

This is bad enough, but when you consider that our children tend to learn their listening skills from us, is it any wonder that they don't listen too well? I always used to think that my children had inherited their poor listening skills from my husband, who for many years has suffered from selective hearing. When I began to get more familiar with my behavioural profile (I'm a Monkey parent), it began to dawn slowly that I might perhaps have something to do with the problem.

An obsession with talking, as opposed to listening, can cause your kids to clam up. We're human and we like to be listened to. If we're not, we'll make ourselves heard in other, less productive ways, which often involve bad behaviour. This isn't good for family life.

From the Mouths of Kids

Sometimes my mum goes on and on. I just wish she would listen to me for a change. She always has an opinion or a solution to offer and sometimes I just want her to listen. It's like she always has to be right. I don't bother to tell her anything any more, she doesn't listen anyway.

Is the teenager who begrudgingly grunts 'whatever' in answer to your every question merely a mirror of your own listening and communication style? Is the toddler who causes mayhem as a way of getting attention a reflection of your impatience and grown-up temper tantrums? If your kids just don't listen, try turning the tables. Start listening to them. I promise that it'll make you more magnetic, there'll be more listening and co-operation from your children, and you'll spin into a virtuous upwards spiral.

Two Ears, One Mouth

So, here's the challenge. Would you be willing to step back and assess how good a listener you are, and what kind of role model you are? On the whole we assume that we listen well – it's just like breathing, isn't it? Or is it? I remember at school constantly being told that I had two ears and one mouth, and should use them in the same proportions! It's probably one of the most useful bits of information I was ever given, particularly in relation to being a mother, because if you want your children to listen to you, you first have to listen to them. If your children ever shout, 'You just never listen to me,' ask yourself how true that accusation is.

Try out this quiz and see how you score.

1. You are preparing a meal in the kitchen when you hear a call from another room: 'Mummy, I need you.' Do you:
   a) cheerfully down tools, wander through into the sitting room, get down on their level and with a smile ask 'What do you need, darling?'?
   b) shout 'I'm busy, come here if you want me!'?
   c) carry on with what you're doing and shout through to the living room, 'What do you need me for?'?
   d) think to yourself, 'What could they possibly want now? I really need to get this tea made,' and ignore them?

2. Your child has fallen over in the street and cut herself. You don't need a medical degree to know that this is a very superficial and non-life-threatening wound. A small plaster will be the biggest medical intervention required. Passers-by, however, could be forgiven for thinking that your child has been mortally wounded due to the rather loud wailing. Do you:
   a) get down on the pavement with her, examine the offending wound in great detail, agreeing with her that it must really hurt and that you can fully understand the need to cry over such an injury?
   b) give her hugs and suggest that an ice cream might make it better, or maybe a special plaster or some such item?
   c) urge her to get up off the pavement, saying, 'It's not too bad, really, look, all your limbs are still intact and there's no blood'?
   d) tell her not to be silly, 'It's only a scratch, jump up and let's get going, look, you'll feel much better if you can forget about it'?

3. When are your children most likely to want to talk to you?
   a) I know exactly when my child will want to talk to me.
   b) I think I know some of the time.
   c) I don't know, I've never really thought about it.
   d) My children never seem to want to talk to me.
4. How often do you spend time sitting with your child having nothing else to do other than focus on them and what they might have to say?
   a) Several times a day.
   b) Once a day.
   c) Rarely.
   d) I have no idea.
5. You're in the car on your way home from school. Your child is telling you all about an incident that happened in the playground at lunchtime between two friends. When she's finished she asks you what you think. What do you say?
   a) You give your informed reply and then ask what she thinks.
   b) You give your informed reply.
   c) You're not sure what to say because you were thinking about what to cook for tea and had tuned out because the story had been rather long and, dare I say it, a little bit boring. You ask her to repeat what she said.
   d) You say, 'Oh, I'm sure they'll all be fine,' as you're not really that interested in playground scuffles.
6. Your child seems moody and whenever he's asked a question he responds with the word 'whatever'. Do you:
   a) find a quiet time to listen to him alone and get to the bottom of it?
   b) empathize, remembering what it was like to feel like that yourself when you were his age?

c) just ignore him, or ask if he knows any other words?

d) tell him to buck up his ideas and lose the attitude?

7. You are asked if you can appear on a reality TV show. A fly-on-the-wall camera will record your typical week and then an expert will watch the footage and feed back to you how good a listener you are. What do you think the feedback will be?

a) You're a fantastic listener with no points for improvement.

b) Could do better but probably no worse than most other people.

c) You could be doing a lot better.

d) You'd be too embarrassed to let the cameras in for fear of what they might record.

8. Your child seems very quiet and withdrawn. Do you:

a) make sure you get some quiet time with her when she might open up to you?

b) question her incessantly about what's wrong?

c) ask her brother what is wrong?

d) assume that she will be OK in the morning and ignore it?

9. If your child had a problem at school, how likely would he be to tell you about it?

a) Very likely.

b) He might tell me.

c) I'd be more likely to find out from someone else.

d) He wouldn't tell me.

10. How much would you say you really know about your children and what's important to them?

a) Excellent, I know everything.

b) OK, I know most things.

c) I don't really know the names of all their friends and what they love about school and life.

d) I could know a lot more if I spent more time listening to them.

The Scores on the Doors

How did you do?

If you got mostly As, well done, you get the Listener of the Year Award.

Mostly Bs? Not bad, but could be better.

Mostly Cs and Ds? Well, listen up, there's some work to be done here!

Spot the Difference

You'll know already there's a real difference between people who listen and people who don't. Take a look at the two conversations below and ask yourself why one of them is better than the other.

Conversation one

'Mummy, Rachel told me that I was smelly today in the playground. I really hate her, she's always saying nasty things to me.'

'Just ignore her. When I was at school people always used to tease somebody. You know what they say? Sticks and stones will break your bones, but names will never hurt you. Anyway, guess what I did today?'

Conversation two

'Mummy, Rachel told me that I was smelly today in the playground. I really hate her, she's always saying nasty things to me.'

'Is she? How does that make you feel?'

'I hate it.'

'I bet you do. Do you want to tell me more about it?'

> *Tip!* Think about the labels you give your children – they might just live up to them.

Answers on a postcard, please

The insightful, intelligent among you will no doubt have spotted that there were a few not terribly subtle differences between these conversations. Obviously, conversation two was better. The mother in conversation two will probably have a better relationship with her child and a bit more respect. Why? Because she's listening to understand, rather than listening to reply like the mother in conversation one.

In conversation two the mother is attempting to listen to what the child is trying to say. All she has done is use a few simple techniques from the world of effective listening.

If you're hanging your head in shame because you're sometimes just a teensy bit guilty of committing listening crimes yourself, worry not: I'm going to give you some tools to turn things around and make you a magnetic listener.

For the next week, every day I'd like you to try out some new listening techniques and see what happens when you do. I think you might just be surprised at the difference they can make.

Listen Up

I know that we take listening for granted, but like many other skills it can be learned, improved and honed. When done properly it can reap amazing emotional rewards. Here's a poem that I think sums up why listening is so crucial – and some of the pitfalls we unwittingly stumble into on a daily basis when listening to our children. The author obviously had a profound sense of how important it is to be listened to, and as a child how frustrating it is if you're not.

> *Tip!* Look for positive qualities in your children and notice out loud when they display them.

Listen

When I ask you to listen to me
and you start giving me advice,
you have not done what I asked.
When I ask you to listen to me
and you begin to tell me why
I shouldn't feel that way,
you are trampling on my feelings.
When I ask you to listen to me
and you feel you have to do something
to solve my problem,
you have failed me,
strange as that may seem.
Listen! All I ask is that you listen.
Don't talk or do – just hear me.
Advice is cheap; 20 cents will get
you both Dear Abby and Billy Graham
in the same newspaper.
When you do something for me that I can
and need to do for myself,
you contribute to my fear and
inadequacy.
And I can do for myself; I am not helpless.
Maybe discouraged and faltering,
but not helpless.
But when you accept as a simple fact
that I feel what I feel,
no matter how irrational,
then I can quit trying to convince
you and get about this business
of understanding what's behind
this irrational feeling.
And when that's clear, the answers are
obvious and I don't need advice.

Irrational feelings make sense when
we understand what's behind them.
Perhaps that's why prayer works, sometimes,
for some people – because God is mute,
and he doesn't give advice or try
to fix things.
God just listens and lets you work
it out for yourself.
So please listen and just hear me.
And if you want to talk, wait a minute
for your turn – and I'll listen to you.

– Ralph Roughton
Clinical Professor of Psychiatry at
Emory University in Atlanta, Georgia

Become an Amazing Listening Machine

So, if you don't want to end up accused of not listening, try out the seven strategies below.

Strategy one – get ready to listen

A bit obvious, I know, but are you really *ready* to listen to your children? Just because your ears are conveniently situated on the side of your head doesn't automatically oblige you to use them. Like the mobile phone in your handbag, they're only any use if they're switched on. From now on, every day, set your intent to listen. Say to yourself, 'Today I am a willing listener. I'm switched on and ready to receive. My children will think of me as a great listener.'

Of course, this might be easier said than done, so how would you ensure that you follow through on this little promise to yourself? If you're like me, you'll know that the things you promise yourself you'll do, like not eat chocolate cake, don't always happen. Your will to follow through often comes down to 'state management'. Are you in the right state or frame of mind to listen?

I know if I've been out at work all day, when I walk in the door the children will want to speak to me. I have to switch out of work mode and into home mode. It's as if I have to turn off the noise in my head about work and clear my head space so I can focus on them and what they want. If I don't, I find it really hard to concentrate on what they're saying.

Your 'state' is how you are at any given moment in time. It changes depending on what you're doing or how you're feeling. Frazzled, calm, focused or distracted are all states you might find yourself in. In relation to listening, there are some useful questions to ask yourself to determine whether you are in the right state to be an amazing receiver of what your child transmits.

I never realized how often I said, 'Just a minute' to my children. My wake-up call came when my four-year-old asked when 'just a minute' was. I'd been fobbing her off for years and she had no real expectation of me being available to listen when she wanted me. Neither did she know when I would be available, because, if I'm truthful with myself, my distracted and unfocused demeanour meant that 'just a minute' never came.

When you think about your interactions with your children, how conducive is your state to listening? Does it assist with your goal to have your antennae switched on, or does it block out the signals coming your way? Just for a moment, ponder the following questions.

When I'm listening to my children:

★ what do I feel like?
★ how do I sound?
★ am I totally focused on what they're saying?
★ do they feel like I'm really listening to them?
★ what do I think about when I'm listening to them?
★ who am I being?
★ how do I behave when I'm listening to them?

Now ask yourself this:

How would I be if I were in a great state for listening?

★ How would I look?
★ How would I sound?
★ What would I feel like?
★ What would be happening?
★ what kind of reaction might I get?

Everyone's list will be different, but here you have your own personal action plan. This is the state that you need to be in so you can be open to hearing what your children have to say. You're clearing away the interference and white noise that get in the way of transmission.

When Will You Be Ready to Listen?
But what if you can't clear the airways? What if you're not in the right state to listen? Perhaps you really haven't got time, maybe you're rushing out the door. If your children want to talk and you can't listen, then postpone the conversation until you can. The important thing is to make sure that you follow up and listen when you said you would.

From the Mouths of Mums

Motherhood and life generally being what they are, I sometimes find that I can't listen when my kids want to talk. They've now learned that if I say I'll listen at a particular time, I will. For a long time, though, I used to say I'd listen later, then never did.

Strategy two – perfect timing

I don't know about you, but I've always found that children don't do much on demand. When I've got time to listen, they don't want to talk, and when I've got no time, talking is the only thing on their mind. There seem to be certain times when my children aren't that interested in talking, and other times when they are. At the end of the school day is a perfect example. I'm always keen to know what they've been up to. My incessant line of interrogation about their day would be great preparation for a job interview, but it took me a while to realize that their reluctance to go beyond, 'It was fine, Mummy' was a sure sign that 3.15 after a long day at school was not one of their favourite moments for opening up. Start noticing when it is that your children like to open up and talk to you.

From the Mouths of Mums

I've noticed that my son seems to like to talk to me about things that are more important to him at bedtime. I don't know why, but it seems to work for him. Maybe because he has my undivided attention and nobody else is listening. I've learned to spend time with him each evening because I can more or less guarantee that this is when any issues or problems at school, or just general information, will come out.

Ask yourself the following questions:

☆ When do my children seem to open up more easily?
☆ Are there times when they don't seem to like to talk?
☆ When is the best time for me to make time to listen to my children?

Becoming more familiar with when your children are likely to talk will give you a much better chance of being able to listen to them. Equally, knowing when they are most receptive to you gives you a much better chance of being listened to as well. Whether it's in the back of the car on the way to school, while you're watching TV with them, in the bath or at bedtime, they'll have times that they prefer to listen and talk. Work out what works for your children and family.

Strategy three – meet them in their world

With the airways clear, you're fully available to receive transmissions. Something that will help you receive loud and clear is if you can really get into the skin of your children and understand things from their point of view, not just your own. If your child is doing exams, can you remember what that was like? If they are trying to learn addition, can you remember what that was like? If they are frustrated with you because you've told them they can't go out until their room is tidy, can you remember what that was like? Put yourself in their shoes for a moment and think about an issue they might have. If you were them, would you discuss this issue with you? If not, ask yourself why this might be. If you've not been the world's greatest listener in the past, what could you do about that now? By starting with a degree of empathy for where they're coming from, you will immediately open up the listening channels. Try this exercise to help.

Exercise: Listen with Your Children's Shoes On
In this simple exercise, you literally step into your child's shoes and become them. Like Tom Hanks in the movie *Big*, momentarily become your child and tune in to their world. When you take on the role of your child, you can better listen and empathize with where they are coming from. It's a wonderful way to help you get on their wavelength, which, if you have teenagers, is quite a feat to achieve! Here's how you do it.

★ Think of the child you want to listen to.
★ Draw an imaginary circle on the floor.
★ In the middle of the circle, imagine that you see the child's shoes.
★ Step into the shoes and imagine that you are now that child.
★ As you stand in their imaginary shoes, look at, think about and hear the world from their perspective. Think about how they experience the world. Think about things from their point of view. As you do, wonder what would need to happen for this person to listen to you. How would you need to behave?
★ Step out of the circle and become yourself again.
★ Now have a conversation with your child, but listen with *their* perspective in mind.

Strategy four – rapport

All this and you haven't even started a conversation yet! But now you're well and truly in listening mode, let's learn about rapport. When you engage in chit-chat, your rapport skills could make or break its success. Do you know anyone who's a great listener? Think for a moment about a time when you were on the receiving end of someone who really listened. You were engaged in a conversation where you felt genuinely understood and heard. A conversation where you felt 100 per cent comfortable and the communication flowed smoothly; you were totally at ease and talked happily and freely. When you're in a conversation like this, you're in *rapport*. In rapport you're on the same wavelength as the person you're talking to. You're more likely to open up, listen and be influenced by the other person. This is why any salesperson will try and create rapport with you the moment you walk into a shop. Sometimes it's difficult for us to get into rapport with our children because we don't seem to know what their wavelength is. Equally, they struggle with tuning in to ours, and this makes it tricky for us to identify with and listen to what they have to say.

From the Mouths of Mums

It upsets me sometimes how well I get on with my friends and how badly I get on with my children. Why is it that conversation flows easily with my friends but quite often ends up in arguments when I'm with my children?

When you're in good rapport it's a bit like driving a sleek precision-engineered car. It's smooth and it runs like a dream. When you're in one of these machines you just want to keep driving for ever. When you're in poor rapport it's like driving an old banger. Everything feels clunky and awkward. The transmission doesn't work and you get frustrated as it kangaroos down the road, eventually grinding to a halt. You can't wait to get out.

Sometimes people feel the conversations they have with their children are the equivalent of a stock-car race, while those that they have with their friends are much smoother. If someone was to eavesdrop on your conversations with your children, would they be like Formula One rallies or something out of *Wacky Races*? If you want to be a first-class racing driver, then check your transmission, get into gear and create rapport.

Take a Look in the Mirror

So how does rapport work? To explain, I'd like you to think back to this morning when you brushed your teeth. Recall for a moment you brushing your teeth in front of the bathroom mirror. I'm sure it's something you've done many times, so it shouldn't be too difficult. But just imagine that you're doing it tomorrow, and instead of your reflection mirroring back what you're doing, it does something different. While you're busy brushing your teeth, your reflection perhaps waves back at you. How weird would that be? Odd as this might sound, when we communicate we tend to feel more comfortable and as if we are being listened to if the person we're with mirrors what we are doing. The communication flows more smoothly and more listening takes place. You only need to look around you to see how true this is.

Exercise

This week, just take a moment to watch people who are deep in conversation and seem to be agreeing and listening intently to each other. Notice in particular their body language. More often than not, if they are in rapport they will be like a mirror image of each other. If one person is leaning slightly forward, the other person will probably be leaning slightly forward, too. If one person has their arms folded, the other person will probably have their arms folded. Are they standing or sitting in a similar way? Something that I always find funny is if you watch people in a café. If they are in rapport, as one takes a sip of their coffee, the other will probably lift their cup and take a sip of their coffee, too. It's like synchronized coffee-drinking. When you start to look out for this, it's amazing how much of it you see. On the whole, people are oblivious to how they mirror each other when they are in a state of rapport.

Also keep your eyes open for people who don't appear to be having the most productive of conversations, and don't look as if they want to listen to each other. You'll notice that their body language is different. They're probably not a mirror image of each other. One may have their arms crossed and the other might be shaking a finger. One might be leaning forward and the other backward. They'll look different from the people who were in rapport.

Mirroring is a wonderful way to create and enhance rapport with your children, and it's not just with body language that we can achieve this. It's possible to mirror people's voice tones, movement, posture and breathing. Of course, you have to be careful not to mimic them, that's not the idea. Sometimes something as simple as sitting next to your child on the sofa in the same position as them will be enough to mirror and start rapport off. Why not try it for yourself and see what happens?

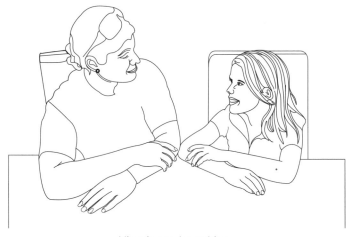

Mirroring and matching

Exercise

Go for a walk with your child. Focus on mirroring them as much as possible, without it being obvious. Walk at their speed, match their footsteps. If they stop and bend down to look at something, you stop, bend down and look, too. Talk at the same pace as them. Notice what changes you have to make to your own voice, posture, movement and breathing to match those of your child. Notice what it feels like when you do, notice how they react to you when you do. This is called *pacing*. Try pacing your child. Like anything you've not tried before it will probably seem a bit odd at first, but stick with it.

Follow the Leader

The wonderful thing about mirroring someone is that you really get onto their wavelength. This helps them to feel more comfortable with you. So much so that they will begin to mirror you without even realizing that they are doing it. So how can you use this to help with listening? It's simple: once you've got great rapport by pacing your child, you can take the lead and they will start mirroring you. As if by magic they

No mirroring and matching

will do what you do. If you are in rapport and have paced them well, they will follow your lead. You become magnetic. Let me give you an example of how this works in practice.

Take a Deep Breath

Mirroring breathing patterns is a highly effective way of establishing rapport, particularly with tiny children who perhaps can't speak. I remember an incident when my youngest child refused to sit in her car seat. She worked herself into such a frenzy that I thought a passer-by might call the police, she was making such a noise. Her back was so rigid there was no chance whatsoever of me being able to strap her into the seat. I had a couple of choices. Lose it, shout and forcibly push her into the seat, or let the tantrum run its course. I chose the latter and used mirroring to help calm her down. Instead of talking to her, I turned sideways so I was in roughly the same position as her and my body was pointing in the same direction. While trying not to look too much of an idiot in the car park, I matched my breathing pattern to hers, saying nothing and adopting the same rhythm as her.

When she took one of those huge breaths that come when you've exhausted yourself with crying, so did I. No words were spoken, but rapport was established through our mutual breathing. After a few minutes of pacing I took the lead and she willingly followed. I turned around, faced her and did up the seat belt, then gave her a big kiss and a hug. I moved us from a downward to an upward spiral by pacing her. When I felt we were in strong rapport, I took the lead. I listened to her, but I listened to her breathing. I did this rather than shouting and trying to force her into her seat.

Another example of this is when my son was adamant that he didn't want to do his homework. Normally he does it without too much complaint, but on this particular day he wasn't interested. He got quite irate and took himself to his room. I left him to his own devices for a few minutes. He's an

Elephant, so I didn't want to rush him. I gave him a moment to process and reflect. When I went into his room, he was lying on the bed staring at the ceiling. Now of course, I could have gone directly into 'preachy parent' mode and said some very unhelpful things:

'If you don't do your homework you'll never get a good job.'

'Sometimes in life we all have to do things that we don't want to.'

'Whether you like it or not, you have to do your homework.'

All three of these statements would have gone no way towards creating rapport – in fact, they would without doubt have diminished it, and sent us back down the success spiral. Tempting as it is to be self-righteous, I avoided this as an approach. Instead, I climbed onto his bed and lay next to him. I didn't say a word and just breathed at roughly the same rate as him. I didn't talk, I didn't do anything, and neither did he. I was just there with him. I waited for him to speak and then replied to him using the same tempo and volume of voice he did. My natural speaking pace is quite fast; his is quite slow and more considered. Only when I felt I was 100 per cent in rapport with him did I suggest that we went down and did the homework together. He took my hand and we went downstairs. Now, notice I'm not saying we skipped down, he still wasn't 100 per cent happy, but he agreed to do what he had refused to do a few moments earlier. I achieved this just by establishing rapport, mirroring and pacing him and then leading. Of course, this approach takes more time, and the temptation is to break into preaching parent. But start mirroring your children and in effect you're listening to them on a whole new level. You're listening with your body, not just your ears.

Really look for opportunities to pace your children. I promise that if you do, it'll reap rewards on the listening front.

From the Mouths of Mums

I realized that barging in front of my children while they were watching the TV and switching it off was never going to create rapport. After learning about rapport, I understood that if I wanted them to listen and turn off the TV, I had to establish rapport first. I now do this by pacing them. When you think about it from their perspective, you can understand why someone snatching the remote would upset them – it'd upset me if someone switched my programme off when I was engrossed. So now, I either give them three warnings so they know it's coming, or I sit next to them and mirror their sitting position so rapport is established before I take the lead and ask them to switch it off. This has eliminated a huge amount of acrimony in our house.

Strategy five – turn off autopilot

Have you ever wondered what it's like being on the receiving end of your listening?

From the Mouths of Kids

I just showed my mum my artwork. She said it was fabulous, but she looked distracted and she only looked at it for a nanosecond before she rushed off. She didn't say it in an enthusiastic way, like she really did think it was good. I know she said it was fabulous but I don't really believe that's what she thought.

Think about it: do you believe the server in the burger bar when he says, 'Have a good day'? Your ears will hear the words, but you only believe them if they match up with the visual signals you get. If he thrusts the burger into your hand and looks fed up to be alive, does he seem as genuine as the smiling, intent person who hands you your tray politely? Is the less genuine-seeming server just on autopilot? Do you sometimes listen on autopilot, and pay lip service to what your children say? When words don't match actions, our other senses kick in and question the authenticity of the other person.

Our children aren't daft; they pick up on when you're not listening because there's a mismatch between what they hear, what they see and what they feel as they process your reaction to their words. Your child's brain is like an interpreter. It takes all the sensory input coming from you – not just what it's hearing but what it's seeing, too. It decodes this data, then draws a conclusion about whether it believes if you're being genuine or not. All this happens very quickly and often on a subconscious level. As adults, we too pick up on these mismatches between what is being said and what we believe to be true.

From the Mouths of Mums

I went to pick up my child from school. He had tears in his eyes and looked quite upset. I asked him what was wrong. His bottom lip started to quiver as he replied, 'Nothing.' I couldn't believe it. There was definitely something wrong, but he kept saying that he was OK.

We pick up a lot of communication signals not just through our ears but also through our eyes. In fact, it has been suggested that when our brain decodes communication, as much as 55 per cent of the meaning we make from it is down to how the person we're listening to actually looks. So things like how they breathe, facial expressions, body posture, movements and gestures tell us a huge amount about what they mean. Your eyes are just as important as your ears when it comes to listening. To prove the point, turn down the sound on the TV. Watch the action and, just with what you can see, try to decode what the characters are saying. You'll pick up a lot even though you can't hear the words. If your children are up for it, try it with them, too. We listen a lot more with our eyes than we realize.

Thirty-eight per cent of the meaning we make from communication is down to how the other person sounds, so the tone of their voice, its pitch and pace will heavily influence what we really hear. Just think of times when you've been abroad and listened in on a conversation in a language that you don't recognize. Quite often you can get the gist of the meaning just from the pitch, pace and tone of the voices.

Amazingly, only seven per cent of communication seems to be made up of what is actually said. I think, on the whole, most of us rely far too heavily on the weight of what we say to get our children to listen to us. We should, perhaps, focus more on *how* we say it. When we do this we get more rapport and more listening in return. So, if your children aren't listening to you, ask yourself if what you are saying is matched by how you look and

Tip! Every day, ask your children what were the best bits of their day.

sound. If you say you're enthusiastic about something, is this matched by your posture, voice and gestures? If not, make some changes – and watch the impact it has on your children.

Strategy six – silence, please

They say silence is golden, but how often do you keep schtum when your children are talking? If your children are telling you something interesting, use silences to encourage them to speak more.

On the whole, most people find it difficult not to jump in and fill up a silence. Use this to your advantage. Instead of filling conversational gaps yourself, encourage your children to say more and let *them* fill the silences. This week, focus on being silent as you listen to your children. See if they drop a bit more information into the pot. It's a great technique for getting children to open up.

Strategy seven – clarification

A young child was sitting at the breakfast table with her father. She asked him this question, as only a four-year-old could:

'Where does poo come from?'

'Um,' replied her father, not quite sure if this was a conversation to be had over cornflakes, but none the less wanting to do his best to give a comprehensive answer to his daughter's question, in terms she could understand. He went on to explain what would happen to the cornflakes she was currently eating and how, as a result of a number of bodily functions, her breakfast would be turned into poo, finishing with the words, 'And that is where poo comes from.'

Delighted with his explanation, he was getting back to reading his paper when his daughter, in a puzzled voice, asked, 'Daddy … what about Tigger and Eyeore, where do *they* come from?'

I bet this father wished he'd just clarified what his little girl was really asking before he'd launched into his graphic explanation!

Clarifying your understanding of what's being said is a really useful way to show that you are listening and to ensure that you've understood what's been said. Try using some of these listening techniques to clarify that you've understood what your children are telling you. Show that you're really listening.

Clarification

Clarify that you've heard correctly: 'You want to know where poo comes from – what do you mean by poo?'

Conversational Summary

This allows you to show that you've listened to and grasped the main things that have been said. It also gives the other person the opportunity to correct you if you've misunderstood:

'I hate football and I hate my new coach.'

'So, what you're telling me is you don't like football any more and you're not keen on the new coach?'

'Well, I don't hate football, I still love football, but the new coach is mean and I'm not enjoying it as much as I did.'

Reflecting Back

With this technique you repeat or reflect back what has just been said. This demonstrates that you've been listening, and it's often a good technique for getting more information from the other person, particularly if you reflect back and leave a silence at the end:

'I hate football and I hate my new coach.'

'You hate football and you hate your new coach?'

'Well, I don't hate football, but I'm not happy about the new coach.'

Elaboration

This is where by asking for elaboration you demonstrate your interest but also collect more information:

'I hate football and I hate my new coach.'

'You hate football and you hate your new coach?'

'Well, I don't hate football but I'm not happy about the new coach.'

'Tell me more.'

This week, look for opportunities to clarify, summarize, reflect or elaborate. We'll be building on these next week, so really try to use them over the next seven days.

Summary

So there you have it: a whole raft of strategies to improve your listening. Don't save them for a brick wall, go try them out on your family. It'll make you more magnetic. They'll notice that you're listening, so they'll open up to you more. Joy of joy, they might even start listening to you. See you next week – and by the way, thanks for listening.

☆ We're often guilty of listening with a view to responding rather than a view to understanding.

☆ If you listen from your children's point of view, they are more likely to open up to you.

☆ By our getting into the right frame of mind to listen and by creating rapport, not only are our children more likely to listen, they are more likely talk.

☆ Listening is more about understanding than speaking. Conversational tools such as elaboration and summary will assist you in listening.

Week Four Actions

★ Each day, set your intention to be a great listener.

★ Notice your state. Get into a great state for listening when you're with your children.

★ If your children bring you an issue or problem, put yourself in their shoes and experience it from their perspective.

★ Create rapport with your children as much as you can: try mirroring, matching, pacing and leading.

★ Each day, try one new conversational strategy such as silence, clarification, summary, reflection or elaboration.

Week Five:
Solution-seeking

Magnetic Principle
Number Five

Focus on solutions, and
problems will look
after themselves

Problems, Problems

Now, I don't mean to be negative, but let's talk about problems. For a parent they come with the territory, don't they? Arriving unexpectedly in an array of interesting colours, shapes and sizes, they present us with a multitude of challenges daily.

From the Mouths of Kids

I can't do my homework.
Charlotte said I smell like dog poo.
I want my nose pierced.
Why can't I go into town on my own?
I don't want to eat broccoli.
Henry ripped my Pokemon card.
She hit me.
I'm not doing it and you can't make me.

Just thinking about this could give you a headache. Dealing with it could give you a migraine. Like a 24-hour news channel, our children have the ability to present us with a continuous stream of issues, disasters and quandaries to be solved. Sometimes they'll be looking for you to find a solution. Sometimes they'll have their own ideas, but these ideas might be a million miles away from what's acceptable to you. Often you end up in conflict, spinning perilously downward as you discuss these ideas and act as the policeman in family contretemps. There are tears before bedtime, possibly yours, and harmony doesn't reign in your house. Sound familiar?

Let's turn our thoughts to how we can deal with such situations in a way that makes it easier for us and also empowers our children so there're dry eyes all round. The way to do this is to focus on finding solutions to problems in partnership with our children. And we're not just talking about any old solutions, but solutions that empower them and leave everybody feeling happy. We also want to teach them how to be independent, resourceful problem-solvers. This is our challenge, so let's rise to it.

The Problem-solving Parent

One of the difficulties I find when coaching parents is that very often they get sucked into their children's arguments and issues. They focus on finding who is to blame, or suggesting their own solutions without involving their children. Like throwing petrol on a fire, they make things worse by becoming part of the problem themselves. They fan the flames of conflict.

From the Mouths of Mums

I realized that, more often than not, I asked my kids what their problem was and why they had it, rather than asking them what the solution might be, which meant we didn't always get very far with finding any. We just kept having the same arguments again and again. It was like a recurring dream – or should I say nightmare?

As a nation we tend to love problems, we love to find someone to blame for them and we love to offer our solutions and words of wisdom. It's a national pastime. Just look at any news headline – they're splattered with problems and misery looking for a scapegoat. We're just as bad with our children: we focus on what they are doing wrong and partake in finger-pointing as we attribute blame. Sometimes, of course, we take the initiative and provide solutions, not retribution, but usually it's a solution that *we've* thought of. We don't tend to involve our kids in finding their own. Foisting blame and your own solutions on your child is very disempowering.

James was being bullied at school, so I told him to ignore the bullies and tell his teacher. It never really occurred to me that he might have some of his own suggestions for solving this problem. I suppose I just thought, 'I'm his mum, I know best.'

In an attempt to help our children we often become their personal problem solvers. Although this is great as a quick fix, it doesn't teach them independence.

As a generation I think we do have a tendency to mollycoddle our offspring. I had to laugh recently when I came across an article in the quality press which seemed to epitomize the excessive problem-solving parent. In the piece it described what I would call an over-zealous parent who, at a prestigious junior horse-riding event, had allegedly fed another pony a 'mint'. It transpired that the mint was perhaps not a mint after all, but possibly a debilitating drug to impair the performance of the opponent's horse. I know it's not funny, but I did chuckle. What a length to go to to ensure your child wins.

In the book *May Contain Nuts*, a problem-solving parent dons a cap and poses as her daughter in order to take an exam for her. Now this of course is problem solving gone mad, and you have to wonder where such behaviour will lead. My guess is it's not a good place.

So how do you solve the domestic issues that arise on a daily basis without being part of the problem yourself, and without weakening your child's problem-solving muscle by solving it yourself?

Solutions, Solutions

On the menu this week we're serving two tasty options to help you to find amicable solutions to any problems that might fall on your plate. Most issues our children dish up fall into one of two categories, and each has a simple process for reaching a solution that won't leave a bad taste in your mouth. When war breaks out in your house, no longer will it be necessary for you to don full body armour as you wade in and get caught in the crossfire. You'll have two secret weapons in your arsenal for dealing with the fighting. These weapons, should you choose to use them, are *Coaching* and *Negotiation*.

Coaching

Definition: 'Facilitating the creation of a solution to a defined problem.'

Coaching will assist you in finding solutions to issues where you and your child want broadly the same outcome.

'Mum, I need some help with my homework.'

This problem fits the coaching bill perfectly. For coaching to work, it's likely that both parent and child will want the same outcome: a great piece of homework.

You might wonder why you'd need a process for this. If you both want the same result, then surely there won't be any conflict? Ever helped a child to learn to ride a bike or do his spellings? Then you'll know that, although you both want the same outcome, it's sometimes easy to foist your views and opinions on your child. As you'll probably have experienced, this can sometimes result in frustration and a downward spiral of communication for both of you.

> *Tip!* When letting your children know what they've done wrong, always be clear that the behaviour *is wrong, not the child.*

*I was really delighted when my daughter asked me to help
her with her German homework. 'At last,' I thought, 'my
schoolgirl GCSE will come in handy.' Three hours, several
boxes of Kleenex and two frayed tempers later, I realized
that helping my daughter had not been as easy as I
thought, even though we both wanted the same thing: for
her to understand German.*

Coaching is an effective tool for helping your child to solve
issues without you necessarily telling her the answers. It's
useful in all sorts of scenarios, and helps your children to
become independent thinkers.

Negotiation

Definition: 'To talk and listen to achieve an agreement.'

This second approach to help you find effective solutions
is useful for the problems that are sometimes more explosive
because parent and child want different outcomes.

*My daughter, who is eight, thinks she should be able to go
to bed at nine o'clock. I think that's far too late, and it's
the source of constant arguments in our house.*

In general, negotiation is most useful as a problem-solving
approach when people want different outcomes. If you feel
like a broken record and repeatedly get stuck in the same old
groove, arguing about the same issue, negotiation could flick
you out of your downward spin.

The Perfect Couple: Coaching and Negotiation

Let's have a look at where these approaches can help.

	Coaching	Negotiation
When to use it	Parent and child want a similar outcome	Parent and child want different outcomes
Typical scenarios	Helping with homework Learning something new like swimming or riding a bike Making a decision Dealing with bullying	Body piercing Getting a pet Going to a sleepover Wearing a very short skirt A new bedtime
A real scenario	Louise has been bullied at school. Your inclination is to go and see her teacher, and sort out the bullies yourself. This, however, is *your* solution. Coaching will help Louise to develop her own solution. Because the ideas come from her, not you, and she owns them, it's more likely to be successful.	Your daughter, who is 8, wants to have her ears pierced. You're averse to piercing of any description. She insists that every other person in her class (including the boys) has their ears pierced. She considers you to have the fashion acumen of a caveman, and considers you as dinosauric as a T Rex for your backward views on the issue. Negotiation might just hold the answer to a solution you can both live with.

Helping Your Children to GROW

Let's first take a closer look at coaching. Coaching is a wonderfully collaborative way to facilitate problem solving. I like to think about coaching like flying a plane, with you as co-pilot and your child as captain. The captain and co-pilot select a destination. In order to fly there, they first establish their current position. That agreed, they can then assess the route options. Once they've decided which way to go, they take off and fly. The pilot makes the decisions, the co-pilot supports. This is a simple four-step process, and problem-solving with children follows a similar pattern.

The GROW coaching model is one of many formats you can use to coach your children (or anyone else for that matter). Originally developed by one of the world's leading executive coaches, Graham Alexander, it's simple and easy to get to grips with. Just like the plane journey, it has four components. Each letter of the GROW acronym represents one part of the coaching model:

Goal	Where do you want to go?
Reality	Where are you now?
Options	How can you get there?
What Next?	What action will you take?

The coach's or co-pilot's skill is to help the captain answer these questions and guide them as they formulate their own answers and solutions.

Will you help me with my homework?

How does it work in practice? Let me demonstrate by sharing the story of a child we'll call Sarah. She'd recently started secondary school. This was a new environment for her, with lots of new challenges, including a raft of unfamiliar curriculum subjects. Also came the new and perhaps daunting concept of homework.

As parents, we want to help as much as we can to ensure our children do their best, so when they ask for help with work, it's tempting to almost do it for them. When Sarah showed her mum the ICT homework she had, the impulse to take over and do it for her kicked in straightaway.

The homework asked Sarah to put together a survey of the items in her house which contained microchips. Sarah was a little uncertain about how she should approach the task. Forgetting it was Sarah's homework, her mother had already started to race ahead, thinking of all the wonderful ways in which this information could be presented. She then checked herself and moved from 'do it for them mode' into 'help them to help themselves mode', which is another way of describing coaching. Instead of suggesting her own solutions and ideas in a directive way and pushing them onto Sarah, she moved to a more supportive role, where she pulled information from Sarah about how she might approach the homework. This mum used the GROW model to support her child in creating her own answers and ideas.

Here's how their conversation went. Notice how the listening strategies of silence, clarification, summary, reflection and elaboration, introduced in the last chapter, are being used in this conversation.

> *Tip!* Use disciplinary and motivational methods that suit you as a parent and your child.

	Conversation	Comments
Sarah	I'm not sure what to do for my ICT homework.	Here we have a problem to be solved.
Mum	What does it ask you to do?	Mum asks a question to establish the **GOAL**. Of course, the temptation here is to take over and be directive, telling Sarah what she has to do. She's also using the listening technique of **clarification**.
Sarah	Well, I think it's got something to do with counting how many electrical appliances we have in the house. But I don't know what I'm meant to do.	Sarah **clarifies** what she thinks she's meant to do, but it's obvious that she still isn't quite sure what's expected. The **GOAL** still hasn't been fully established.
Mum	OK, let's think about it for a moment. What do you think it's asking you to do? What is your teacher expecting you to hand in?	Mum asks another question to **clarify** the **GOAL**. Again, she resists the temptation to wade in with her solutions and suggestions, but asks good, open questions to get Sarah to come up with a definition of what she thinks the **GOAL** is.
Sarah	Well, I think I have to count all the appliances in the house that have got microchips inside them. Write them all down and hand it in by next Tuesday.	

Mum	Is it asking you to do anything else? Mum now remains **silent**.	Mum asks another question which gets Sarah to **elaborate** and **clarify** if there is more to this **GOAL**. She's attempting to get Sarah to come up with her own interpretations rather than pushing forward her own. Asking a question like, 'Is there anything else?' is a good way to get Sarah to **elaborate**. Also keeping **silent** at the end of the sentence means that she's giving Sarah a chance to speak. If Mum doesn't fill the silence, then Sarah probably will.
Sarah	Well, it says it's got to be creative.	It worked: Sarah **elaborates** and fills the silence beautifully.
Mum	So you need to come up with a creative way of showing how many items we have with microchips in them?	Here Mum uses **summary** and **clarification** of the **GOAL**. It's a great way to show that you're listening and that you've understood what the other person is saying.

Tip! Plan in a time every week that is sacred family time. Invent family traditions and celebrations.

Sarah	Yes.	Sarah now knows what the **GOAL** is. Sarah established this herself by answering her mum's questions. She's gone from feeling unsure to sure about what she's expected to do. Mum wasn't directive. She pulled the information from Sarah by using effective listening strategies and asking good questions. Now, you can move on to the next part of the model, which is to establish **REALITY**, or current position.
Mum	So what have you done so far?	This is the 'Where are we now?' question. Mum is checking the facts of the situation. What's been done already? What's our current position?
Sarah	I've made a list of all the items, but it looks really boring – it's not very creative.	Sarah tells her mum what she's done so far. The **REALITY** is established.
Mum	So, you've made a list and you think it looks boring. So what if you did something that didn't look boring and was creative, what do you think that would look like?	Mum **summarizes** the **REALITY** and then moves on to **OPTIONS**. By asking what the finished product might look like, she's asking Sarah to think about what she might have to do to achieve her **GOAL**, and encouraging her to give some ideas or **OPTIONS**.

Sarah	Well, it could have pictures. I could cut and paste pictures of different appliances into the document to jazz it up a bit. I could use different fonts, too.	Sarah willingly provides a number of **OPTIONS**.
Mum	That's a great idea. Anything else you could do?	Mum asks for more **OPTIONS**. Mum is resisting the temptation to offer her own suggestions.
Sarah	Well, I'd quite like to make it like a leaflet, one that folds out with a different room shown in each section. I could have the appliances shown room by room.	Sarah provides another of her own **OPTIONS**.
Mum	That's great. Anything else you can think of?	Asks for more **OPTIONS**.
Sarah	No.	OK, no more **OPTIONS**.
Mum	So, if we just look at the homework instructions again, if you do what you've said will you be happy that you've answered the homework question?	Mum **clarifies** that Sarah is happy that what she's proposing will be sufficient for the homework.
Sarah	Very happy.	She's happy, so let's move on to Step Four: **WHAT NEXT?**
Mum	OK. How are you going to do it, then? What software do you think you'll use?	Agree a way forward by deciding **WHAT'S NEXT**. Mum is asking Sarah for actions.

Sarah	Well, I could use Excel and then sort the spreadsheet by room.	
Mum	Tell me more.	Mum asks Sarah to **elaborate**.
Sarah	Well, a table in Word would probably work, or maybe even Publisher. I'll just have a play around and see how it goes.	
Mum	Great, do you need any support from me?	Only at this point does Mum offer her support with the implementation of Sarah's ideas.
Sarah	I'm fine, I'll call you if I need you.	Sarah is now able to go off and do her homework. Job done!

The only support that Sarah required was to scan in a couple of pictures. She produced a fabulous piece of homework which was 100 per cent hers and earned her two merit marks.

This is a perfect example of a coaching scenario, magnetic parenting and the upward spiral all in action together. Of course, the conversation could have gone quite differently.

A Conversation without Coaching

	Conversation	**Comments**
Sarah	I'm not sure what to do for my ICT homework.	
Mum	Give me the question and I'll have a look.	

Sarah	OK.	
Mum	OK, it's asking you to count up all the electronic items with a microchip, then make a chart to represent them. Now, the way I would do it would be as a table in a Word document. I'd use a box for each room and then list the items. Just run round and count up all the things we have with a chip, then write it into the table. You could even use a few different coloured fonts just to jazz it up a bit. Sound OK?	Here Mum provides all the solutions for Sarah's problem. Sarah has no input and is not empowered. You also have to wonder what she will learn from the homework doing it like this.
Sarah	OK, but I'd like to try doing it in Excel so I can sort the data by room.	
Mum	Oh no, I think Word would be much better. Do you know how to do it in Word?	Mum isn't listening.
Sarah	Sort of.	
Mum	OK, well wait until after dinner and I'll come and set it up for you.	After dinner, Mum produces a wonderful piece of homework that has Sarah's name on it. She got one merit mark!

Why does coaching work?

I hope it's self-evident why coaching works. When you ask children coaching questions to help them work things out for themselves, it's amazing what they come up with. In the Sarah scenario, you can see that in a coaching interaction she was empowered to make decisions, and encouraged to be creative and to put forward her own ideas. Her mother was non-judgemental. How magnificent does it make a child feel to come up with her own ideas and have them taken seriously? Children are so used to be being told what to do, they're often stunned when asked for their opinion, but I never cease to be amazed at their resourcefulness. For me, the success of coaching is based on your ability to do just two things: to listen and to be curious. You learned how to listen in the last chapter. Developing your curiosity and asking the right questions of your children mean you'll find they know a lot more of the answers to their problems than you possibly gave them credit for.

Curiosity Never Killed a Coach

It might have killed some cats out there, but to my knowledge curiosity has never killed a coach. So get curious with your children and feel safe to use these killer questions in coaching conversations. They'll really help you to facilitate the process of empowering your children to develop their own solutions to their own problems.

Get Curious about Goals

★ What do you want?
★ How will you know you've got it?
★ If you had a magic wand and everything were fixed, what would be happening?

Get Curious about Reality
* ☆ What have you already tried?
* ☆ What's the current position?
* ☆ What's making you feel this way?
* ☆ What do you think about this?
* ☆ How do you feel?
* ☆ What's happened so far?

Get Curious about Options
* ☆ What else could you try?
* ☆ What are your options?
* ☆ What ways could we solve this?
* ☆ What do you think your teacher/hero/friend would do in this situation?
* ☆ If anything were possible, what would you do?

Get Curious about What Next?
* ☆ What will you choose to do?
* ☆ What are the action steps?
* ☆ What do you need to do next?
* ☆ When will you do this?
* ☆ What are we agreeing is going to happen?

By asking killer questions like these you'll get so much more from your children as they open up and answer them, solving all their own problems. It's like magic.

Coached kids are empowered kids

I'm so convinced by the power of coaching that I believe using this approach can lead to children producing superior results than if the parent tells them what to do. Here's an example of what I mean. It shows how reading can be improved by using coaching and no formal instruction. I've used this many times and it really is effective.

Ask your child to read a passage from his book. Ask him to give himself a score out of 10 for his reading. This score represents the REALITY, or the current position that child believes his reading to be at. I've found it's rare that a child will give himself 10 out of 10.

Next, ask him to identify what he did well and what he thinks he could do better. This further establishes the REALITY or current position.

You then ask him to say what score he would like to get out of 10. This is his GOAL. Usually this is a higher score than he originally gave himself. So a child who said he was an 8/10 reader might, for example, say he'd like to be a 9/10.

Then, ask the child to suggest what he would have to do to be a 9/10 reader. Encourage him to come up with all sorts of suggestions, and OPTIONS that will help him achieve this GOAL. Ask him to continue reading, but as if he were a 9/10 reader. Ask him to read the book doing all the things he suggested would make him a 9/10. It's often astounding the difference in the quality of reading that you hear. Here are a couple of examples of what I mean.

Parent	Let's hear you do some reading.
Child	(Reads a passage from his book.)
Parent	Thank you very much. I really enjoyed listening to that. What do you think was really great about your reading?
Child	(Sometimes a bit surprised by this question!) Well, I took a breath at the full stops and I sounded out the words I didn't know.
Parent	Yes, you did, didn't you? I noticed that you were doing that. Doing that really helps make your reading sound lovely to listen to. So, what mark would you give yourself out of 10 for the reading you just did?

Child	I'd give myself 7/10.
Parent	7/10. I'm curious to know: if you could give your reading any score out of 10, what score would you like it to be?
Child	Well, I think I'd like it to be a 10/10.
Parent	10/10? That's a great goal. What would you need to do to be a 10/10 reader?
Child	Well, I'd need to use more expression.
Parent	Anything else you'd need to do?
Child	I don't think so.
Parent	So, if you used more expression you'd be a 10/10 reader. OK, then, how about you do some 10/10 reading for me? How do you feel about that, would you like to try it?
Child	Yes.
Parent	Off you go, then.
Child	[The child reads and usually this will be in a much more fluid way, and you can usually see and hear that he is putting more effort into what he is doing and focusing on what he said he wanted to improve. In this case, using expression.]
Parent	Well, thanks for that. What did you think of that reading, what was good about it this time?
Child	Well, I put in more expression.
Parent	What mark would you give yourself for that reading?
Child	I think it was 10/10 reading.
Parent	And what's it like being able to do 10/10 reading?
Child	Really good.

Of course, there's always the possibility that a child may think he is already a 10/10 reader. So where do you go with that, how do you stretch him? Get curious about his reading and ask some great killer questions. Questions like these:

Parent	Who is the best reader you've ever heard?
Child	Stephen Fry. I love listening to him read *Harry Potter*.
Parent	What would you need to do to read like him?
Child	Well, I'd need to slow down and really pronounce my words well.
Parent	How about we read like Stephen Fry?
Child	OK.

And so it goes on. Coaching really is a powerful tool. Don't be afraid to use it.

Call in the Peace Corps

Coaching works, we love it, and it's a great way to get your children to co-operate without having to lumber them with your solutions, but what happens when you both want *different* outcomes? First of all, check the availability of Kofi Annan. My bet, if he's not too busy negotiating a Middle East peace deal, he'll feign illness in order to avoid involvement with your negotiation, as it'll probably be much more difficult and challenging than his normal daily work. Chances are you'll have to roll your sleeves up, take a deep breath and get on with it yourself.

Negotiating is a lot like coaching in some respects, so you're halfway there already. There's just one main difference: when it comes to examining options, things can get a bit sticky. This is because what you want is likely to be vastly different from what your child wants. If we think about the plane analogy again, it's like the co-pilot and pilot wanting to fly to different destinations. Somehow you've got to mutually agree on a compromise destination.

I visualize this conundrum like a ladder up against a wall, with the parent at the top of the ladder and the child at the bottom. The goal is that the two people have to somehow agree on an outcome in the middle. The problem is usually that neither of them wants to move from their position on the ladder. That's where the conflict and downward spirals start. To get to this middle ground, the two need to compromise, which requires some movement up or down by each of them. If you've been struggling to make that happen, here are a few pointers.

Negotiate with Style

Let's use bedtime as an example. I'm sure it's the source of conflict in many a household. Your eight-year-old wants to go to bed at nine o'clock. You think that eight o'clock is fine. Immediately your GOALS are mismatched. There's a gap between what your child wants and what you want. The REALITY in this situation is that you have a happy parent who thinks the current bedtime is fine, and an unhappy child who wants to change it. In negotiating it's what's termed as a 'win/lose' situation: parent wins, child loses. What you want to achieve is a 'win/win' outcome, so that both parent and child win, and everybody is happy.

Now, it might be that you think eight o'clock is the correct bedtime and you're not prepared to negotiate. You're not willing to move down the ladder to meet your child. This is what's known as a stalemate, and you choose to walk away from the negotiation before it has even started. Of course, you could argue that this is a great place for children to learn the harsh realities of life. They can't always have exactly what they want. It's OK some of the time to say 'No,' but if you want your kids to enter the real world believing that every time someone says 'No,' that's it, remaining immovable every time they ask for something is a great way to do it. Wouldn't it be better if they were equipped with a set of skills that enable them to articulate what they want, feel empowered to go for it, and make a stab at getting it? Negotiating is a life skill. When you think about it, is Mum saying, 'No, you can't have a dog' any different to being told 'No, you can't have that pay rise?' Do you need a different set of skills to deal with each? Not really. Demonstrate 'win/win' negotiating skills to your children and they'll get the hang of it from watching you.

Now, I'm not saying that you should negotiate every little thing with your children – that would be madness – and I talk about boundaries and rules in the next chapter. But there are ways of discussing options so that some movement up and down the ladder of negotiation takes place to ensure both parent and child achieve a 'win/win' outcome.

Tips and techniques of top negotiators

Most of the potential conflict in a negotiation will arise when it comes to agreeing the middle ground. Establishing the GOAL and REALITY are usually pretty straightforward, but examining options and agreeing on one when you both want different outcomes is where a few negotiation tactics can come in handy. Using bedtime as an example, here are a few tricks and techniques from the world of negotiation to use when considering options and to get some movement up and down that ladder so you can meet in the middle and reach an acceptable agreement.

Your daughter currently goes to bed at eight o'clock. She wants to go to bed at nine o'clock. You're happy with an eight o'clock bedtime.

How Far Are You Prepared to Go?

Before beginning a negotiation, always know what your bottom line is, or how far you're prepared to go before you reach your walk-away position. Let's pretend that in reality you'd let your child go to bed at 8.30, but no later. That's your bottom line. By knowing your limit, you know exactly what you have to bargain with. You have a whole 30 minutes.

Keep Your Cards Hidden
They say information is power. So when you know your bottom line, don't blurt it out straight away. As soon as your child knows 8.30 is a possibility, they'll push for 8.40 and you'll have no more to give because you went to your bottom line too quickly and removed all your options.

Start Low and Work Up
Your child wants an extra hour, you know that you're prepared to give another 30 minutes. In the negotiation, when you're bargaining, start with a low offer so you've got room for manoeuvre. For example, your opening offer in the negotiation might be, 'I'll let you stay up until 8.10.' You know your child will probably push for more, but you've still got a whole 20 minutes up your sleeve. Of course they don't know that, and if you subsequently give them more time they'll feel that you're being generous and they've got something from you.

Bargaining
If you make an offer of ten minutes, don't expect them to bite your hand off. They want nine o'clock; you're 50 minutes away from their ideal. You'll have to start bargaining. Good job you kept those 20 minutes in hand. The key to negotiation is bargaining. When there's a bit of give and take from both parties, it somehow seems fair and is more likely to end up in a 'win/win' outcome. It gives you the potential to go up and down a ladder rather than round in circles. If she wants more than ten minutes from you, what is she prepared to bargain with, what is she prepared to do for you? Will she move up her ladder a bit and perhaps move by ten minutes too, to 8.50? Bargaining will bring you closer together.

Concessions and Counter-offers

You've just moved one rung down your ladder. You've conceded ten minutes. OK, it's not a lot, but you've shown willing. Now your child needs to make a concession and move a bit closer to you – what we call, in negotiating terms, the middle ground. Achieve this by asking her what she's willing to do for you.

'If I let you go to bed later than 8.10, what are you willing to do for me?' Use the great negotiating phrase: 'If you do this then I'll ...' This tactic is a great way to move both parties one rung closer to each other, because you each make a small concession.

You'll be surprised at what your child comes back to you with. Perhaps she'll tidy her room, take the dog for a walk or empty the dishwasher. These offers might make it worth your while to move a bit more. The empty dishwasher might make it worth offering an 8.20 bedtime.

What Else Can I Bargain With?

Negotiation isn't always just about the matter in hand. I used to work with estate agents teaching negotiation skills. One of the things I emphasized is that negotiation isn't always about the most obvious thing. In the case of a house sale, the negotiation isn't always about price, although it's easy to think that it would be. Other factors come into play, for example how quickly the sale can move through or the readiness of a buyer to wait a period of time before moving in. In the case of this negotiation it doesn't need to be just about bedtime. When you limit yourself to this one topic, the negotiation can

Tip! Use natural consequences as a fair way of learning about life.

get to a stalemate quite quickly. You'll hit an impasse because you've run out of places to move.

So think about what might float the boat of your child. If you don't want to move her bedtime, what else could you give her instead that would result in a 'win/win' outcome for you both? Why does she really want her bedtime moved? Maybe she wants a later bedtime so she sees more of Dad, who gets home late. Would special time with Dad in the morning or at the weekend be something she'd like instead? Widen your **OPTIONS** by thinking of other things that are attractive to your child, not just the immediately obvious issue.

The Creative Compromise

Are there ways you can offer options but not have to give in completely? For example, maybe she could go to bed at nine on Saturdays and 8.15 on weekdays. Think about alternative options that could work for you both.

Trial

How about going for a trial period? See how it goes and take it from there. Perhaps you agree that 8.20 is the new bedtime. You agree to trial this for three weeks to see how it goes. If your child seems fine and is getting enough sleep, perhaps you'll review it again.

Beware of Red Herrings

Children will throw these into a conversation randomly. The best advice is not to rise to the bait – ignore them.

'It's not fair.'

'All my friends have it.'

'I'll never speak to you again.'

'You're always picking on me.'

'I'd rather have Charlie's mum than you.'

Agreement and What's Next

Always end any negotiation in the same way you end a coaching conversation, with an agreement about what's next. What's been decided, who will do what and when? It's important that you get clarity with agreements.

'Your new bedtime is 8.20. We will start that from next Monday. You will be allowed to stay up until nine on Saturdays, and one day a week Daddy agrees to come home early to put you to bed. Are we agreed?'

This is important, because if the bedtime creeps to beyond 8.20 you can always refer back to this agreement.

Be Prepared to Meet Again

If you can't reach an agreement, set another date to talk again. At least this way you're more in control of and prepared for the conversation.

Negotiating in action

To demonstrate how negotiating and coaching work in action, I'd like to share with you the curious incident of the dog and the hamster. Like most children, mine have always hankered after an animal, the bigger and more time-consuming the better. This is a topic for negotiation. It's an easy place to say, 'Mum knows best and you're not having it' – a 'win/lose' scenario. Here's the conversation that took place in my house when I was repeatedly asked for a dog.

Child	Mummy, could we have a pet?	
Mum	Exactly what pet is it you're after?	Always find out what the other person actually wants. Clarify their **GOAL**.

Child	Could we have a dog?	In my mind I'm screaming, 'No, no dogs, not in this house. I don't have the time or the patience for a dog. There's no way we're having a dog.' This is my walk-away point, but I need to move down my ladder and bring them a few rungs up theirs so we can perhaps meet in the middle.
Mum	Well, a dog is quite a commitment, what about something easy, like a goldfish?	Counter-offer, so I'm keeping the discussion open and I'm giving something (OK, I know a fish isn't much, but it is something and it moves me a rung down my ladder).
Child	Oh, Mum, goldfish don't do anything, they're really boring. It's not fair, all my friends have got dogs.	Red-herring alert. Clearly it's *not* the case that all their friends have dogs and that it's not fair. Two throwaway remarks. I won't rise to the bait. I'll ignore them and continue.
Mum	I know you'd like a dog, but it's not really something that I can cope with right now. What might be some other options?	At this point I'm summarizing her position, but I'm not saying 'No.' I'm giving her an opportunity to come down her ladder a little bit. I'm asking her to bargain and make a counter-offer.
Child	A cat?	She's come down, but not far enough.

Mum	Well, it's a bit better than a dog, but still quite a commitment. What about something that you can take complete responsibility for?	Acknowledge her movement down the ladder, and ask an open question to elicit an option from her about something else that might be more appropriate. I'm still not saying 'No,' but keeping the conversation open.
Child	OK, a hamster. I can keep it in my room and look after it and you'll never have to even touch it.	We're in middle ground now. I'd be happy to settle on a hamster, but I'm not going to say so yet. I want to add in a few conditions. If I give her this, what is she prepared to do for me?
Mum	I'd be willing to consider a hamster if I know that you definitely would look after it. I don't want to have to do anything because I'm not keen on them. So, if you can prove to me that you know how to look after it and you can save up to buy it, I'll think about it. If you can prove to me that you can do that, in a month's time you can have a hamster.	I'd be willing to give you a hamster if you do something for me.

Tip! *Make time for yourself every day.*

Child	Yippee! Oh, Mummy, I love you.	I'd like to think that she loves me anyway, and it's not conditional on the purchase of a rodent, but hey, it sure feels nice to be able to say yes and end in a scenario where everyone feels happy.
Mum	Let's put a date in the diary for four weeks from today. If I'm happy that you can do what's necessary to look after the hamster, then you can have one. Just talk me through what you need to do to get the hamster.	Clarify the agreement and what happens next.
Child	I have to research how much they cost and how to look after them. Then save up enough to buy it and a cage.	Everybody understands what the agreement was and what has to be achieved in the next four weeks.
Mum	Let's put a date in my diary to talk about it next month.	

What happened next? We had our chat four weeks later. My daughter had kept her room tidy, she'd researched hamsters on the Internet, had worked out where she'd buy a cage from. She had, in fact, become a hamster aficionado. She'd also negotiated with her brother and sister to split the cost of a cage, food and bedding, and agreed that they were to share the responsibilities of caring for it. What could I say, other than 'Yes'? She'd kept her side of the bargain. Now, 18 months on, the hamster is still with us and the children have complete responsibility for him. When we go on holiday or away for a weekend, they take responsibility for finding someone to look after him. I've been delighted by their resourcefulness and also by the fact that, as yet, I've never had to touch the animal, probably more to its relief than mine.

What could have happened?

Child	Mummy, could we have a pet?	
Mum	I've told you before you're not having a pet because I know who'll end up looking after it, me.	
Child	Please Mum, can we have a dog? Everyone else has got one.	
Mum	Not everybody else has; in fact, I'm struggling to think of anyone who has. Now please stop asking about dogs because it's not going to happen.	
Child	You're really mean.	

Kids That Can

I'm a great believer that when you do all these things with your children, it changes the way they operate in the world. It makes you more magnetic and them more resourceful. For me the story I'm about to share is testament to the power of coaching and negotiating, and the results they can produce.

The tamagotchi triumph

Do you remember the craze that hit the world in 2005, the Tamagotchi? Tamagotchis were intensely irritating electronic pets that became the constant companions of your children. (I suppose I only had myself to blame for my children's obsession with cyber-pets, as I wouldn't let them have the four-legged variety.) If you hadn't managed to get your child an electronic pet by normal retail means, you were doomed to pay hundreds of pounds on eBay to secure one of the remaining two in the world, ensuring that Santa didn't fall empty-sacked down your chimney.

If you don't remember, let me remind you what Tamagotchi ownership entailed. It was the bearer's responsibility to keep the Tamagotchi alive and attend to its every need 24 hours a day, seven days a week. This included tasks such as changing its cyber-nappy, exercising it and taking it for walks. Needless to say, this round-the-clock care meant that where your child went, the Tamagotchi went, too.

On the 4th January 2005, 15 million children arrived for the first day of spring term with their Tamagotchis in tow. As they bleeped their way through lessons, headteachers around the land banned the Tamos from their classrooms. The kids were outraged – this was tantamount to murder. Tamos everywhere expired and millions of mothers, who of course have nothing better to do all day, became the custodians of the banned toys while their children were at school.

My children were devastated. Who had to deal with the fallout? Me! I was barraged by an outraged daughter. I have to say I was on the side of the headteacher. I could see clearly her predicament and worry. Let's face it, why do we do the school run every morning? Surely in the hope that our wonderful offspring might learn something at school, not be disturbed by Tamagotchi alarms.

So what did we have here? I was in agreement with the head. My daughter and her friends wanted Tamagotchis back in the school. Seemingly an impasse situation. This presented me with a wonderful opportunity to assert my parental authority, agree with the head, and applaud the Tamagotchi ban. But no, instead I went to the local phone box, donned a red cape, put a pair of pants over my laddered tights and emerged as Coaching and Negotiating Mum. Here's how the Tamagotchi tussle was resolved using collaborative, solution-focused problem solving – and everybody, including the Tamagotchis, lived happily ever after.

The Conversation

Child:	We want Tamagotchis in school all the time; it's not fair.	Ignore the red herring and focus on the **GOAL** she wants to achieve.
Mum	Well, let's just look at it from the head's point of view. Why do you think she's banned them?	Establish the **REALITY** or current position.
Child	Well, because they make a noise and annoy the teachers and we look at them instead of looking at our work.	
Mum	So, what if you did do your work, they didn't make a noise and they didn't annoy the teachers, how would that be?	
Child	Well, that would be fine, I think.	
Mum	So, how could you make that happen?	Request **OPTIONS**.
Child	Well, if we all switched them off during class and only played with them during breaks, that would solve the problem because nobody would be annoying the teachers.	

Mum	That sounds great, so how do you convince the teachers that it's a good idea?	Ask for more **OPTIONS**, while actually resisting the temptation to say that the head is right.
Child	Well, we could put a petition together. Everyone is really annoyed about it, and that'll get the head to listen to what we've got to say.	
Mum	Anything else?	Keep asking for more **OPTIONS**.
Child	We could try and meet with the headmistress to talk about what we want.	
Mum	So what will you do?	With some options established, ask **'WHAT NEXT?'**
Child	I'll ask my friends what they think tomorrow.	
Mum	Let me know how you get on.	

The next day at school, my daughter's friend came up with the idea of writing a letter to the headteacher requesting a meeting to outline their case. Here's what they composed at her house, with a bit of coaching input from her mum.

Tip! Stick to defined boundaries and don't be afraid to enforce them.

Dear Headmistress,

On the 5.01.05 you banned Tamagotchis. There are lots of people who are upset about it. My friends and I have a suggestion, which we hope you don't mind us putting forward.

A letter would be given to all class teachers, who in turn would pass them out to all pupils who have a Tamagotchi. The letter would state that it is the pupil's whole responsibility and not the responsibility of the school. The pupil would sign the letter and return it to their class teacher. We would of course only 'interact' during break times.

We would both be very happy to discuss this further with you face to face and show you the benefits of Tamagotchi.

You will soon be receiving a list of all the names of pupils who do not want Tamagotchis banned.

Yours sincerely …

If I ever needed confirmation that a coaching approach is empowering for a child, the following chain of events was undeniable proof.

The Meeting
The headteacher, a supportive and forward-thinking lady, was very receptive to the girls and had a meeting with them as they requested, in which she listened to their concerns. They were able to consider her objections and put forward

the benefits of their idea. Between them they came up with an agreement and a 'win/win' solution. Here's the extract from the school newsletter on 12th January.

Electronic Games and Tamagotchis

Many children received Christmas gifts of electronic games and Tamagotchis. At the beginning of term I told the children that these should not be brought into school as they have a habit of starting to bleep in the middle of lessons, which is very distracting for the teacher and, more importantly, for the children's learning.

However, I have since received a very polite and well-composed request from a group of children requesting that they be allowed to bring in their Tamagotchis, with the clear understanding that they should be set to 'sleep' during lesson time and that the children would interact with them during break times only. The children have written that they are prepared to sign a letter which will state that the toy is their responsibility and not the responsibility of the school. However, if they do disturb lessons or cause any disputes over ownership, we will reserve the right to take them away from your children and return them at the end of the day to be taken home permanently.

The agreement letter will be sent home on Friday ....

My daughter and her friend were considered the heroines of the day, and if that wasn't enough the local press got hold of the story and ran this piece the following week.

The Paparazzi!

Here we see an almost textbook application of problem solving gone right, and the upward spiral in action. Tamagotchis

EVEN VIRTUAL PETS ARE FOR LIFE

A pet is for life, not just for Christmas – which is why a local school has taken the unusual step of introducing a Tamagotchi Care Agreement.

The hand-held cyber critters have been a popular gift this Christmas and the children have been bringing them into school to give them round-the-clock care as many electronic pets have ended up in cyber heaven after they were entrusted to forgetful parents.

The pets need almost constant attention and beep and burble away to alert their owners to their needs.

The school headteacher said: 'I told the children in assembly that the school could not be responsible for the Tamagotchi if it got lost or broken in the playground and some of the children came to me afterwards and suggested the care agreement. I thought that was a brilliant idea.

'I think it is better to do this than to ban them from school completely. The parents would have to take them to work with them and then they would be beeping away in the office.'

Any pupil who breaks the agreement could see their pet sent to the virtual doghouse.

The conditions set out by the agreement, which every child and their parents have to sign if they want to bring the little creatures to school, are:

1) It will remain in my school bag or drawer during lesson time
2) It will be set to silent or pause so that it does not disturb my learning in lessons or the learning of my classmates
3) I will play with my Tamagotchi at break and lunchtime only
4) I understand that the school cannot take any responsibility for my Tamagotchi if it is damaged or lost
5) I will make sure that I can identify my Tamagotchi so there are no disputes over ownership.

If the conditions are broken, the Tamagotchi will be taken away and returned at the end of the day when it will go home permanently.

Extract from *The Herts Advertiser*; reproduced with permission.

might not be the most important subject matter on the planet. But when your children go out into the world, how fabulous will it be for them if they can make things happen because they know how to get solutions to real problems? Everybody wants to change something in the world. This approach gives your children the skills to do it. So go for it, use coaching and negotiation to focus on solutions and watch your children GROW.

Summary

☆ We have a tendency to focus on who is to blame for a problem, or to solve our children's problems for them rather than focusing on solutions.

☆ If we can encourage children to solve their own problems, it empowers them.

☆ Two approaches that help us to do this are coaching and negotiation.

☆ Coaching is useful when parent and child want the same outcome to a problem.

☆ Negotiation is useful when parent and child want different outcomes to a problem.

☆ A useful model to use when coaching or negotiating is GROW. In this we use questions to establish a Goal, the current Reality of the situation, possible Options for solving the problem followed by an agreement of What's Next.

☆ Asking appropriate questions at each stage of the process is a great way of allowing children to create their own solutions.

☆ In a negotiation, use appropriate bargaining strategies to achieve a 'win/win' outcome for both parties.

Week Five Actions

★ Use the GROW model at least once this week to help your children solve a problem. If you feel yourself wanting to provide solutions or advice instead, ask your children the question, 'What do you think?' Help them to create their own solution.

★ If you're presented with a problem to which you and your children want different outcomes, try a spot of negotiating. Go for a 'win/win' outcome.

Week Six:
Kiss Bad Behaviour Goodbye

Magnetic Principle
Number Six

Good behaviour comes
from consequences
and responsibility

Why Do They Do It to Us?

By this point you have an armoury of self-development and parenting tools that should have led to an upsurge in your popularity at home, as you've transformed from manic to magnificent. And none of it has had anything to do with altering your children's behaviour; it's all been about you. If you've been applying what you've learned, then you'll have noticed a huge improvement in both yourself and your family. The tools and techniques associated with the upward spiral really work. But I do live in the real world, and I know that children still misbehave at times, no matter what strategies you employ.

So what do you do if, despite having applied magnetic motherhood methods to your daily routine, your child still stops dead in the middle of the supermarket and screams his displeasure at your lack of willingness to fill the trolley with a multitude of items from the pick 'n' mix? What behaviour strategy do you employ as you notice you're holding a handful of your own hair freshly torn from your head? Worry not, by the end of this chapter not only will you have more understanding about why children misbehave, but, more importantly, you will be well equipped with some great ideas for turning that bad behaviour round and getting some good stuff in its place. Read on and find out how it's done.

If you're going to turn around any behaviour, and using all the methods we've tried to date isn't working, then you need something else to tackle the problem. The first step towards achieving this is to have an understanding about why it's happening in the first place. Although on the surface it may seem that your children have a personal vendetta against you and a devilish determination to turn those few tufts of hair that still remain prematurely grey, it's important to remember that children can behave badly for a number of reasons, and not just to send you to an early grave.

Child Style and Parent Style

Think back to Week Two when we looked at behavioural styles. How your child is born and has a natural tendency to behave plays a large part in the behaviour equation. Equally, how you are will have an impact. The Lions, Monkeys, Elephants and Owls of this world will all behave in different ways, but we've already covered that, so what else might have an impact on their behaviour?

Attention

Children love attention. If there's no positive attention, they'll take whatever's going, even if it's negative. In their eyes, some attention is better than no attention. We already know this, too. In Week Three, we looked at how to make our kids feel magnificent. When you give lots of positive attention, it encourages good behaviour. In fact, the giving and taking of attention is one of the most basic and powerful tools you have to influence your child's behaviour. If you're not giving positive attention, they'll take negative – and how do they get it? By being naughty. Let's face it, when children are being naughty we usually do give them full-on, in-the-face, loud attention. It might not be particularly positive as we rant and rave at them about their latest misdemeanour, but nevertheless attention it is. Quite simply, most of our children have learned a very effective strategy for getting us to take notice of them: being bad works.

Changes

Children often know more than you think. They have the most finely tuned antennae. Because we don't always give them credit for having a pair of ears and a discerning sensibility for what's going on around them, we don't expect them to pick up on environmental and social changes that are happening in the family or life generally. They notice what's going on. Has Dad been made redundant, is Auntie Jayne very ill, are you moving house or getting divorced? You might not have told the children about these changes, but they may very well have picked up on them. It can make them feel uncertain, and this can manifest as bad behaviour. If there's bad behaviour afoot, ask yourself if there's anything happening in the family or at school that might be unsettling your child. This could be the root of the evil.

We're Meant to Break the Rules

Finally, I think as a mother you just have to accept that children will break the rules for no other reason than, like all humans, they like the idea of exploring possibility. We are programmed to break the rules. Think about it: to explore possibility you have to be prepared to take a risk, to overstep a boundary. The only way you'll ever know if a boundary really exists is if you test it out. As a species, humans are naturally curious. The great discoveries and breakthroughs of our time have most often come about through the sheer determination of someone to push a boundary or question the status quo. Bannister's four-minute mile, landing on the moon and climbing Everest, to name but a few, are all boundaries that were pushed by determined, curious humans. It's human nature to push boundaries in order to facilitate our growth and personal development. I'd be worried if my children didn't try to break the rules occasionally; it's a mark of human progress.

Are You a Rule-breaker or a Rule-follower?

What about you? Are you always on your best behaviour, or do you break the rules occasionally? I bet you do, don't you? Just like your children, you too can be bad. Just to be clear, that's what bad behaviour is: overstepping a boundary or breaking a rule. Doing something that somebody doesn't want us to. Just for a moment, think about when you break the rules. It might just contribute to your understanding of why your children also break them, and what you can do about ensuring they follow them.

Consider what you'd do in the following scenarios.

1. You are in a hurry to get to an important appointment. You have three junctions of the motorway to go, it's very quiet and there's no traffic. You think if you drive between 80 and 90 mph you'll get there on time, but if you stick to the speed limit you'll be about ten minutes late. *Do you break the speed limit, yes or no?*

2. You are in a hurry to get to an important appointment. You have three junctions of the motorway to go, it's very quiet and there's no traffic. You think if you drive between 80 and 90 mph you'll get there on time, but if you stick to the speed limit you'll be about ten minutes late. There is also a police car behind you. *Do you break the speed limit, yes or no?*

3. You are in a hurry to get to an important appointment. You have three junctions of the motorway to go, it's very quiet and there's no traffic. You think if you drive between 80 and 90 mph you'll get there on time, but if you stick to the speed limit you'll be about ten minutes late. There is also a police car behind you. You already have six points on your licence. *Do you break the speed limit, yes or no?*

In my experience, when people answer these questions they reply 'yes' to the first question. They are happy to break the rules of the road provided they don't think that they'll get caught or that what they are doing is dangerous. In other words, there isn't likely to be a consequence or penalty for their out-of-order behaviour. As the possible consequences become more severe and more likely to be enforced, fewer and fewer people answer 'yes' when asked if they would speed.

Life Is a Game of Consequences

So here we see the most important element that comes into play when engendering great behaviour: it's called consequence. Discipline is a game of consequences. It's also a game of two halves: reward and retribution. Most things that we do will have consequences. These consequences will be negative or they will be positive. Essentially it's the theory of cause and effect. Every action we take has a resulting reaction or consequence. In essence, when we teach our children how to behave, we're teaching them about consequences. If you overstep the line, there are often negative consequences; if you toe it, there are often positive consequences. So, often what will influence a child's behaviour is one of the following:

☆ Is there a negative consequence? Will I get caught and punished if I don't follow this rule?
☆ Is there a reward or positive consequence if I follow this rule?

Like you on the motorway, they are in total control of their actions. What influences their behaviour are the possible consequences.

What to Use, Carrot or Stick?

Now, of course, parents always want to know what kind of consequences they should put in place to ensure that their children choose to behave in an appropriate way. Should they use reward or retribution? Do we dangle a carrot or brandish a stick? Well, I guess this depends on your perspective and where you think your children are coming from. Back in the

1960s Douglas McGregor, a psychologist, came up with a motivational theory. It proposed the notion that there are two basic styles of managers, Theory X managers and Theory Y managers. I always say that I think parenting is very similar to being a manager, so this theory is useful in thinking about how you motivate your children to behave as you want them to. Instead of Theory X and Y managers, I like to think about Theory X and Y parents. These two types of parents have slightly different views about how to motivate a child.

Theory X parent believes:

☆ Children don't like to do things and will avoid doing anything at all costs.
☆ Children need to be forced and controlled.
☆ Children need much direction and need to be threatened and coerced into doing things.

Theory Y parent believes:

☆ Children want to please you.
☆ Children are creative and like to solve problems.
☆ Children want responsibility and like to be involved in problem solving.

You'll have picked up that Theory Y parent's attitude reflects pretty much everything we've covered in this book. To me, the mindset of the Theory Y parent is most helpful when thinking about how to discipline children. It's my belief that children don't break rules because they are bad, they do it because they are normal. They are creative, inquisitive, intelligent beings. More often than not, they test boundaries to determine whether they are real. A child will only know a boundary is real if they've tested it to see what kind of reaction they get when they overstep it. A boundary that is enforced with a consequence makes them feel secure. A boundary that is consistently enforced encourages children to take responsibility for their own behaviour.

From the Mouths of Mums

I always told my children that they weren't allowed to take food or drink upstairs. I was really bad at doing anything about it if they did, to the point where I found it impossible to stop them from doing it. To be honest, there didn't seem much point in having the rule because nobody ever took any notice of it and it was a waste of my breath trying to stop them.

If, like the Theory Y Parent, you believe that children are fundamentally good and they want to be good, you can begin to weave theories of motivation that reflect this in your parenting.

Where Do I Start?

Sometimes it's difficult to know where to start. There are so many different behaviours you might want to change, and often they're just little niggly ones, like the children not putting their washing in the basket. But they do all add up, and when you're not sure what to do it can seem overwhelming. With that in mind, I'd like to introduce you to a simple and incredibly useful model that I've used for years. It works brilliantly with children – though, interestingly, I didn't learn it in the world of motherhood. I learned it from the world of

Tip! Notice how many times in a day you tell your children not to do something. Instead, tell them what you would like them to do.

business. As a manager looking after staff, I usually found that when people were working with me, they'd behave in one of three ways. They'd be doing things that I liked and I wanted them to *continue* doing. They'd be doing things that I didn't like, that I wanted them to *stop* doing. Or they'd not be doing things that I wanted them to *start* doing. Basically, their behaviour – good, bad or ugly – would always fall into one of these three categories.

You'll probably find that it's the same with your children: there are things you want them to stop, to start or to continue doing. The model I'm going to explain to you contains strategies for dealing with each type of behaviour, and is, unsurprisingly, known as the *Stop, Start, Continue* Model. It really couldn't be any simpler.

Let's look at each type of behaviour in a bit more detail, then think about how you can use the model to get more of the behaviours you want from your children, and fewer of those you don't.

Stop, Start, Continue

Stop behaviours

As the name cunningly suggests, *stop* behaviours are behaviours that you want your children to stop doing. Whether it be biting, bickering or backchat, you'd really rather they didn't do it. For me the most interesting thing about a *stop* behaviour is that, on the whole, a child can choose whether he does it or not. Like you with the speeding on the motorway, it's something that children are in total control of. For example, they could *stop* leaving their clothes on the floor, they could *stop* arguing about when they do their homework, they could *stop* leaving their shoes in the kitchen if they wanted to. If they exercised their freedom of choice, they could *stop* all sorts of behaviours. The trick is making it worth their while to *stop* these behaviours and *start* doing something else instead. We'll be looking at how you can influence them to make the right choice and *stop* doing things that you don't like.

Start behaviours

Start behaviours are those that you'd like your children to start doing. The key thing about a *start* behaviour is that quite often these probably won't be activities that your children will necessarily want to do. You'll probably never have a problem with the *start* behaviour of 'Play on your Game Boy,' or 'Watch the TV.' Usually it's stuff they don't want to do, like putting their shoes on the rack, doing their homework on time and picking the clothes up off the floor. You'll be pleased to hear that we'll be looking at ways to motivate your children to do these things.

Continue behaviours

Continue behaviours are the behaviours that we most often neglect. Why? Because, on the whole, we're so pleased that our children are doing what they are supposed to, we don't think to notice it. You may have experienced this at work.

From the Mouths of Mums

I never really thought about it before, but I like to be told I'm doing a good job. My boss doesn't give me feedback unless something goes wrong, and then he can't wait to have a go at me. I suddenly realized I was doing the same with my children.

For me, the majority of good behaviour comes from encouraging what's being done well. You get what you focus on, so focusing on the good stuff will help to ensure that it continues. Before you knew the power of the success spiral, my guess is that you were focusing on what you wanted your children to *stop* and *start* doing. I'm hoping that for the past few weeks you've been encouraging positive behaviours by wearing your 'Magnificence' specs from Week Three. This week we'll be looking in more detail at how you can encourage your children to *continue* doing what they are doing well.

The human traffic light

So how can you use the *Stop, Start, Continue* Model in practice? Well, to get the behaviours you want from your children, you have to become like a human traffic light. By identifying the good, the bad and the ugly, you can get clarity about what changes you want to see. As a starter for ten, capture the behaviours you'd like to pay attention to. What do you want your children to *stop* doing, what do you want them to *start* doing, and what do you want them to *continue* doing? In the grid below, categorize your children's behaviours into the three areas.

Behaviours I'd Like My Children to:		
STOP	START	CONTINUE

Next, I want you to take one behaviour at a time and work on a strategy for getting more or less of it.

> *Tip!* Make time every day to spend quality time with your children. Plan it if necessary.

Getting more of what you want – continue behaviours

I'm going to start with *continue* behaviours, because it's the area of discipline that we neglect the most. You really do get what you focus on, and this is a really easy way to get more good behaviour. This week, make a real effort to pay attention to behaviour that normally you might take for granted. Instead of catching your children doing something wrong, catch your children doing something right, then praise them for it. Here's how.

Praise Them, Praise Them

Like David Attenborough on safari, stealthily creep through your home keeping your eyes peeled for that wonderful sight: your children doing something that they're actually meant to be doing. Perhaps they're sitting quietly and playing nicely with each other. Maybe they are emptying the dishwasher or making their bed (I know this might be hard to imagine, but try anyway). Approach them quietly so as not to disturb the happy scene, and quickly praise them for what they are doing right.

Giving Good Praise

Tell them specifically what it is they are doing that's good, and the positive consequences of the behaviour: 'Thank you for all playing together so nicely and for sharing your toys so well. I feel so happy when you do that, I think I might even join you.'

'Thank you for putting your shoes on the rack. It really makes a difference to me.'

At all costs, avoid the temptation to be sarcastic: 'My goodness, I'm surprised that you know where the shoe rack is, you use it so rarely.' Comments like this will *not* encourage them to do it again.

The approach works because it uses the motivating assumptions associated with the Theory Y parent: that your children are intrinsically good, and eager to please. They will do more of what you reward them for. They are naturally creative and want opportunities to do well. So, giving attention to good behaviour will encourage more of the same. It's an easy strategy, so why not catch your children doing something right, starting today?

Getting going on start behaviours

What about *start* behaviours? If getting children to start doing something were easy, you wouldn't need this book. The truth is, in order to start a new behaviour you need a little motivation. Let's face it, if the task were something your children wanted to do, they'd be happily doing it already. I imagine that most of the things you'd like your children to start doing are as unappealing to them as a poke in the eye with a sharp stick. Tasks such as tidying their bedroom, clearing away washing or completing homework are not desperately appealing. Yes, I'm sure your list of desired *start* behaviours is as depressing as piles to them. And, to be fair, if you were your children you'd probably prefer not to start doing any of them either. So how on earth do you get them to co-operate and get on with these behaviours?

There are four elements to starting a new behaviour. First of all you've got to secure an agreement. A little like a work contract, you both have to sign on the dotted line and make an agreement about how to approach the new behaviour.

There needs to be some incentive for your children to complete a task, and some consequence if they don't. Again, it's just like being at work. If we fulfil the obligations of our contract, there are a number of positive consequences – usually we get paid, for a start. You need to have the same form of motivation or positive consequence in place for your children.

With the basics sorted, the next question is, can your child actually perform the task you're asking them to do? In the workplace, if we don't have the skills and knowledge required to undertake a task, we get training until we reach the required level of competence. If you want your children to empty or stack the dishwasher, you have to teach them how to do it.

Finally, the fourth step is feedback. How are they doing with their new *start* behaviour? Just like the performance appraisal at work lets you know how you're progressing, feedback will let your children know if what they are doing is OK, or needs to be done differently.

Here's how you implement these four steps.

Step One – Agreement

☆ Select one of the *start* behaviours from your list. Let's say, for argument's sake, it's emptying the dishwasher. Pick a time when you think your children will be in the mood to listen. With your newfound coaching and negotiating skills, make a proposal about the behaviour you want to see started. Negotiate and coach your way to an agreement. Avoid the Judge Dread 'I am the Law' approach. If you want your family to agree to the new behaviour, you'll need to get their input.

☆ Agree what is going to happen and when it's going to happen. Check that everyone understands. Be very specific about what the agreement is. Who will empty the dishwasher and when? Once a day, twice a day, in the morning or in the evening? Do you want it done as soon as the washing cycle completes? Your children may think it's fine to wait until you've completely run out of dishes before they open the door to unstack the now urgently required cups and plates. Be specific in your expectations. This is particularly important if you have a Monkey child or if you're a Monkey parent.

★ To avoid disputes, write down the agreement for the new behaviour and place it where it can be seen. When it's in black and white, it's hard to argue with.

★ Set a date when the new routine will commence. It's important to give your family a bit of time to get used to the idea of the *start* behaviour. This is particularly so for Elephants, who need time to adjust to the idea of change. Begin a countdown to the day the new behaviour is scheduled to commence. For example, remind them that from next Monday they will be emptying the dishwasher, not you.

★ Make sure all the tools required are available.

Step Two – Motivation

The consequences and rewards for engaging in a new behaviour will form a major part in the agreement. The carrots that you dangle will entice your kids to jump to it and get going. Also, the negative consequences of not doing a job will play a part in their willingness to perform. Let's first take a look at rewards, the goodies you can bestow upon your children for a job well done.

Soft Rewards

Soft rewards are those that have no tangible asset associated with them. Praise, as described earlier in this chapter, is a good example. In a world full of children who expect and see much materialism, soft rewards cannot be underestimated. Encouraging your children to do a good job for the sake of doing a good job is a great thing. Do they really need to be given an iPod for remembering to empty the dishwasher once? Allowing them to feel pride in their own work – not just because they'll get something but because they feel a sense of personal accomplishment – is a great thing. So use praise copiously.

Hard Rewards

These are the tangible items that you as a parent have the power to giveth and taketh away. There's a simple equation that goes with these rewards. Abide by the agreement and the child gets these. Break the agreement and he won't. The list of rewards you can negotiate with is endless, and the appeal of each will to some extent depend on your child's age. For something to be motivating it needs to be appealing to your child.

Remember what we did way back in Week Two on behavioural styles? Some motivators will appeal more to certain types than others. A teenage Monkey girl will probably be more excited by extra talk time on her phone than an Owl, who might prefer more pocket money. But here are a few to get you thinking.

- ☆ Time – there are all sorts of ways you can use time as a motivator. Time with friends, time on the PC or TV, bedtime, phone credit time, play time, golden time with you.
- ☆ Privileges – using Mum and Dad's PC, borrowing Mum's shoes, having a TV dinner on a Saturday, staying up late at weekends. Think about what your children really like and would want.
- ☆ Money – pocket money is a biggy. From about the age of five, children understand it. It can be a great motivator. It also teaches them the value of money and the link between work and reward. Some people say it's bribery to give children money for jobs. The way I view it is that the economic model our world is built on uses monetary reward as a motivator, so better get them used to it sooner rather than later.

Cumulative Rewards

These are also great and can be encouraging. Star charts work for smaller children. Collecting some type of token or a points system can be helpful too. You really can get quite creative in how you present these rewards, with special charts. I met a parent who had a toy car that they moved round a home-made track every time their child did his chores. When it got to the finishing line, he got to keep the car. Needless to say, this child was car-mad and it was a great motivator.

Remember, age will influence the reward. Younger children will need almost instant rewards as they don't have the capacity to see too far into the future. Also bear in mind their behavioural styles. Elephants and Owls like tick lists. For Lions you might want to add a competitive element. Can she get six stars in one day? For Monkeys, think about how you can make the tasks and rewards fun.

Step Three – Training

I know when I started work I went on a six-week training course before I was let loose on a client. In fact, I struggle to think of any profession where there isn't some degree of training and support given to the 'rookie'. From bricklayers to brain surgeons, there's a training programme that's coupled with supervision and support. Without training, how can you expect people to know what they're meant to do? It's the same for children. If you want them to keep their room tidy, show them what you expect and teach them how to do it. If you want them to hang up their clothes, show them how to use a hanger and how to fold clothes properly. Don't assume they will know. Support is essential at this stage. Remember, what's obvious to you might not be so obvious to them. When

Tip! Never make threats that you won't follow through on.

they empty the dishwasher, do they know what they are sup-posed to do with the plates? Invest time in making sure they understand exactly what they need to do.

From the Mouths of Mums

*I really wanted my daughter to start tidying her bedroom. It suddenly occurred to me after seeing the **Stop, Start, Continue** Model that if I wanted her to start doing things I had to be clear about exactly what I expected, and I had to show her what to do. There also needed to be some kind of feedback for her once she started to do it, so she'd stay on task and keep motivated.*

Step Four – Feedback

With training complete, the time has come for the new behaviour to commence. Your job now is to assess the quality of the work and give feedback. In my experience of working with many people, this is the piece of the jigsaw that's always forgotten. Have you ever worked for a boss who never gave you any feedback? You slogged your guts out and got no rec-ognition or constructive support? Apparently, 70 per cent of people cite their boss as the key cause if they leave their job. Don't make yourself part of the problem in your house, give constructive feedback – or, as I like to call it, *feed-forward*.

How to Give Feed-Forward

If a good job has been done, then tell your children. For feed-forward to be useful they need to be told specifically what was good or not so good about what they did so they know what to do next time.

'You put all the forks in the fork section of the drawer and all the knives in the knives section. I love it when they're all in the right place.'

A good dollop of feed-forward that also includes praise is a great thing. How about getting your kids to give themselves a pat on the back, too? When they do a job, ask them how they feel about it. Do they think they did it well? Get them to evaluate and praise their own performance so they get positive feed-forward not just from you, but from themselves. This is great for their self-esteem. If they haven't done the job properly, give them constructive feed-forward so they know what to do next time. We have a tendency to focus only on what they've done wrong. Make learning your focus, support them and tell them what they need to without judgement or blame.

'Thanks for emptying the dishwasher. I noticed that the cutlery was a bit mixed-up. Can I just show you where each item goes so you know where to put them next time?'

From the Mouths of Mums

We have a family meeting each week. It only lasts ten minutes, but everyone says what they've been up to, what they've done well and what they will do better next week. We then award a little silver cup to the person who has had the best week. It's great for keeping us all focused, and a brilliant way to give feed-forward. It's also the time we dole out pocket money.

Putting a stop to unwanted behaviours

A few years ago my son told me a joke he'd learned at school.

'What do you call a deer with no eyes?'

'I don't know. What do you call a deer with no eyes?' was my reply.

'No idea.'

Tip! Allow plenty of time to do things so that you don't become unnecessarily stressed by your children.

This, of course, was funny the first time, but after 30 times the novelty wore off. It no longer made me laugh. I can't tell you how relieved I was when he came home with a new joke. The point I'm making is that, to stop unwanted behaviours, you can't nag or reprimand because, just like the deer joke, eventually it has no effect. Your nagging just keeps getting louder and longer until you or your children crack. It's only when you get to cracking point that your children realize you mean business, so it's only at this point they'll do what you ask. Constant nagging also ensures that you're paying attention to *bad* behaviour, and as you get what you focus on, this isn't a great strategy. So if you're like an old dog and you need a new trick, I've got a few up my sleeve. Don't listen to anyone who says you can't learn them.

Boundaries

Boundaries or rules are a key component when it comes to *stop* behaviours. Like rules, boundaries provide structure and help to create a model of the world in which we know what to expect from ourselves and from others. Speed limits are boundaries; they tell us how fast we can drive and what speed others should drive at. When we know what to expect, we usually feel safer and more secure. Without boundaries the world wouldn't make sense, and people would do what they liked. We'd have anarchy and it wouldn't be such a great place to live.

Although your children will undoubtedly protest at your boundaries of no food upstairs or no TV before homework, secretly they need and want them. I know it's hard to believe, but honestly it's true. By setting clear boundaries around the behaviours you want your children to stop, you're actually doing them a favour.

Think about it like this: if you compare life to a game of tennis, can you imagine how you would feel if you turned up to play a match and, throughout the game, the rules and court boundaries kept changing? How hopeless would your attempt to play probably be? Rules and boundaries are essential. If your children cause chaos by overstepping a boundary, what should you do so they *stop* doing it? Here are a number of strategies I'd like to share with you.

Stop Strategy One – Ignore Behaviours Beyond the Boundary

If you want your child to stop biting, bickering or whinging, withdrawing your attention from them when they do it is a good strategy. However, not paying attention to bad behaviour isn't always easy. For example, your angels are screaming and scrapping in the back seat of the car while you try to remain sane and drive. The sound of *The Wheels on the Bus* rings in your ears and they're kicking the back of your seat, which drives you mad. If you need to ignore them and keep your cool, try The Magic Cloak technique:

1. Imagine for a moment that you are a superhero with super powers to match. (Let's face it, being a mum, you need them.)
2. Using your power, throw an imaginary invisible cloak around you. Nobody else can see this, but you know it's there. It's like a secret force-field into which no screaming, scrapping or snotty noses can penetrate.
3. Enjoy being calm and untouchable underneath your protective cloak. From inside your cocoon, you can ignore the mayhem outside.

Using this technique, you will notice a feeling of inner calm as you detach yourself from the situation. You will feel less necessity to react to or be involved in irritating situations.

Stop Strategy Two – Don't Nag, Feed-forward

If you think about it, telling-off as a way of trying to change behaviour is pretty ineffectual. Just for a moment, think back to a time when you were told off. It could be as a child or more recently. Ask yourself:

☆ How did I feel about the telling-off?
☆ How did I feel about the person who did it?
☆ Did I change my behaviour as a result?

From the Mouths of Mums

I remember when I was a child being told off because I'd gone round the corner. I was only four and I really got shouted at. I didn't know what I'd done wrong. I didn't know what 'round the corner' meant.

Now think about the last time you told your child off. Perhaps it was this morning when he didn't get out of bed or didn't put his shoes on fast enough.

☆ How do you think your child felt?
☆ How did your child's behaviour change as a result of your reprimand?
☆ How did you feel about the way you spoke to your child?
☆ Given the chance, would you have done anything differently?

Most of us feel a tad remorseful after we've told off a child, and wish we hadn't done it. Often it's just a way of us venting our own frustrations rather than an effective strategy to stop a behaviour we don't like.

A Good Telling-off

If you want a child to stop something, she needs to get some clarity on why and what she needs to do instead, or what you want her to start doing. There has to be an element of reflection and learning – this is so often missing in many a telling-off. Without it, the feedback that you give is pretty worthless. When an element of learning and reflection is incorporated, the behaviour is much more likely to change. A telling-off in the nicest possible way will help a child to change. In a good telling-off there is no blame attributed to the child. The focus is on learning from the behaviour or mistake rather than focusing on what the child did wrong. The behaviour is separated from the child. It is assumed that the child is more than the behaviour itself. Most importantly, it leaves the child knowing what she needs to do without impacting her self-esteem. Here's how you do it.

1. Decide whether the misdemeanour really warrants attention. Be careful not to make mountains out of molehills.
2. Always deliver feed-forward at the time while it's still fresh and the learning can be extracted. Do this in a calm way, as emotion often leads to a downward spiral. You're more magnetic when you're calm.
3. Use your rapport skills. Go directly to the child and pace him as much as possible.
4. Tell them specifically what he has done: 'You ripped a book.' Focus on the behaviour. Don't make identity or personality statements like 'You are a naughty boy.' This is unhelpful as it labels the child.
5. Tell him the consequences of his behaviour, for example how it makes you feel, or that the book can't now be read by others.
6. Extract the learning by asking the child what he needs to do differently. It might be as simple as not ripping any more books. If he's not sure, give him some reflection

time, perhaps in a special place or his room, and ask him to come and tell you when he has worked out the learning.

7. When the learning has taken place, give your child a hug. Let him know that it's his behaviour that's unacceptable, not him. This will leave him with his self-esteem intact.

Stop Strategy Three – Natural Consequences

The key to effective discipline is not retribution but learning. One of the best ways your children can learn to stop doing something is through the application of *natural consequences*. Using the natural law of cause and effect is often much more effective than any punishment you might dish out. It works on the simple principle that every action has a resulting reaction or consequence. You eat too much food, you get fat. You throw a stone in the water, it creates ripples. You don't wear your raincoat, you might get wet. As a method for stopping behaviours you don't want in your children, allowing natural or logical consequences to run their course is a marvellous tool.

From the Mouths of Mums

I'd just dropped my children at school and settled down to my work at home when I got a phone call from my son, who'd forgotten his PE kit. Without it he wouldn't be able to do PE and he would get a detention, neither of which he was very happy about. He wanted me to bring it in. I'd already done it once that term, and had made it clear that I wouldn't do it again. I told him that I was really sorry, I couldn't bring it in, but I would support him in developing a new way of remembering how to take in the right equipment each day. The learning that was reinforced was that he needed to get his things ready the night before.

If you want your child not to do something, let her learn from the natural consequences of her actions. If she knows what the consequences are, she is then in control of her own destiny. Get agreement on what the consequences for inappropriate behaviours will be. If your child knows she is supposed to phone you if she's going to be later from a friend's house than originally planned, the logical consequence associated with not calling is that perhaps next time she doesn't get to go to her friend's. If her bedroom's a mess and there's a surprise invitation to a sleepover, the consequence might be that you are very happy for her to go, but only when her bedroom is tidy. This might make her late. These are the natural consequences of her behaviour.

Make consequences realistic and implementable. 'No friends round for a year' isn't really sensible, and neither will you be able to follow through on it. Natural consequences put children in total control of their own destiny. They can keep on top of their room, they can choose to phone you. This is empowering and a great life skill. You can dish out consequences like organic food: they're guilt-free and good for your children.

Don't Send Out a Rescue Boat
The downside of natural consequences is the temptation to bail out your children. It takes a great deal of resolve to follow through, particularly if you're an Elephant or a Monkey. Ultimately, your children won't thank you for it in the long run. We've all come across the child who gets away with everything – he turns into the kind of child we all love to hate. If you're tempted to capitulate, think to the future. What will be the long-term consequences of letting your children overstep the boundaries? It's not your job as a parent to be your child's best friend. Sometimes as a parent you have to make hard calls to ensure that learning takes place. Think of it as tough love.

Tip! Whatever you do, ask yourself 'Am I being a great role model for my children?'

Hang Up Your Nagging Hat

So there you have it. How to kiss bad behaviour goodbye. By making an effort to focus on the good stuff, we get more of it. By being clear about what we want and what we don't want, our children know the rules of engagement. They know exactly where they stand. With the right motivation, they are eager to please. The trickiest thing? Not crumpling and sending out a rescue boat when they do overstep the mark. Give your children responsibility for their own behaviour, and you might be pleasantly surprised by how soon you can kiss bad behaviour goodbye.

Summary

☆ Children behave badly for a number of reasons, but not because they are bad.

☆ To encourage children to behave, we need to use consequences. These can be positive or negative.

☆ Children's behaviour can be placed into one of three categories: those you want to *stop*, those you want to *start* and those you want to *continue*.

☆ By paying attention to behaviours you want to continue, you will get more of them.

☆ To get children to start a new behaviour, there are four steps to be followed. Agree the behaviour, agree a positive consequence for adopting the behaviour, teach them how to do the new behaviour, and give feed-forward on how it's being carried out.

☆ To get children to stop doing something, ignore the behaviours you don't want. Give feed-forward which incorporates an element of learning so the child knows what he needs to do in future. Always focus on the behaviours, not the child. Use natural consequences to encourage good behaviour.

★ Avoid the temptation to rescue your children from natural consequences that they have brought on themselves.

Week Six Actions

★ List all the behaviours that you want your children to *stop*, *start* or *continue* doing.

★ Devise a strategy for each, starting with the continue behaviours.

★ Implement your strategy for behaviour change.

Week Seven:
Time Management for Manic Mums and Dads

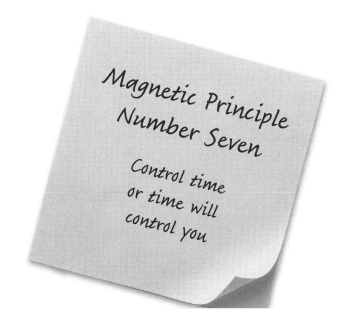

Magnetic Principle
Number Seven

Control time
or time will
control you

Like chocolate, world peace and nails that don't break, we all want more time, don't we? We want more 'me time', and absolutely everybody wants more quality time to spend with their family. Note the use of the words *quality time*. We can all spend time with our children, but is it meaningful? I recently heard that, on average, stay-at-home mums spend 13 minutes of quality time a day with their children. I don't know about you, but most of us could spend 13 minutes trying to get them to brush their teeth, and, believe me, that's not a quality activity.

What about you? How much time are you really spending with your children?

If you've applied the spiral philosophy to your parenting, you should find you've got more time to be with them. With less time wasted chasing them round and incessantly arguing, not only will you have more time but it should be slightly more pleasant. The question is, how do you make your ration of 1,440 minutes or 24 hours a day really count? How do you ensure you're spending enough time with your kids, and making every moment magical?

The answer lies in the Seven Truths of Time Management. Apply them to your family and you'll be amazed at the time transformation you'll experience.

There Is No More Time

Truth Number One is that *there is no more time*. The meter is running and the sands of time are slipping through your fingers as we speak. Most of us don't take that much notice because we think there's plenty left. But is there? Do you really know how much time you've got? How many hours do you think there are in a year? You'll probably be surprised when I tell you that it's only 8,760. Did you know if you lived to the age of 100, you'd have been on the earth for less than a million hours? Doesn't sound a lot, does it? People often say that time is money. I disagree. Unlike money, you can't save it until tomorrow. Each day you get your quota. There's no getting away from the fact that you have to spend your 24 hours every day. There is no more time.

I think about life like a giant egg-timer. The glass domes represent your life, and the sand inside represents the time you've got on the planet. The sand in the bottom dome represents the time that has already passed, and sand in the upper dome is what you have remaining. If you had to guess how much time you've got left, how would you distribute the sand? How much would be in the top dome, time left, and how much would be in the bottom, time spent, time you can't get back?

Most people are usually surprised by how little time they think they've got left, and by how quickly what they've already used has disappeared. I know I was. That's why I like to think about the sand in my egg-timer not as sand but as gold dust. It's the world's most precious resource. Sorry, Marilyn, I beg to differ: diamonds are not a girl's best friend, time is – because, without it, life is worth nothing.

They grow up so fast

Ask any grandmother if she thought her children grew up too quickly. I've never found one who's said 'No.' How many people have tossed this old cliché your way: 'Make the most of it, they'll be grown up before you know it'? It's true. Your time with your kids really is limited. How much time do you think you've got with your children? Have a guess, how many hours? If you take out the time they're at school, and an average of 10 hours' sleep per night from birth to 18, you're left with 48,900 hours. Surprised by how few it is? I know parenting doesn't stop when they hit 18, but believe you me, by the time they get there your ability to influence them will be diminished. If you've done a good job, they'll be truly their own people by that point.

The test of time

So how much time do you spend with your children? Take the 'time test' to find out. In the tradition of Tom Hanks in *Big* or Jamie Lee Curtis in *Freaky Friday*, I want you to pretend that you are your children for a moment. Step into their shoes and answer the following questions as if you are them. It'll give you a great insight into how much time they think you spend with them.

	Agree	Partly Agree	Disagree
I think that my parents spend enough time with me.			
My parents know what I like to do with my spare time.			
My parents are usually available when I need them.			
We spend family time together.			
I can tell that my parents really enjoy the time they spend with me.			
I get enough one-on-one time with my parents.			
I have special memories of things we do as a family.			
My family does things in a leisurely way; we're not always in a rush.			
I feel like I am a priority in this family.			
Although my parents work, they still seem to be able to fit in family time. It doesn't seem to suffer.			
I never sense that my parents are frustrated by having a lack of time.			

As you answer these questions, how do you feel inside? Do you want to jump up and pat yourself on the back because you feel like the world's greatest parent, or do you feel a pang of remorse at not spending as much time as you'd like with your offspring?

Use the scale below to measure how you feel. The lower end represents feelings of discomfort and the upper end represents feelings of comfort. Circle where you think you fit. Now circle where you'd ideally like to be. If the two numbers aren't the same, notice the gap. How big is it? How far away are you from feeling totally comfortable about how much quality time you spend with your children? How would it be if you were spending your desired amount of quality time with them? What would it be like if you were a 10? Now there's a thought. So how do you do it?

Very Uncomfortable									Very Comfortable	
0	1	2	3	4	5	6	7	8	9	10

The Family Eye of Time

The first thing to do is get clarity about how you spend your time right now. If that isn't quite as you'd like it to be, develop a plan that reflects more accurately what you'd like to be doing. To help with this I like to use a tool called the 'Family Eye of Time'.

Here's how it works: just like a real eye, it allows you to see what you're doing at any given moment in time and create a picture of what your quality time profile looks like in your family. It gives you a snapshot of what you're focusing on and how you choose to spend your time.

> *Tip!* You can pick up all your children's stuff, or you can teach them how to do it themselves.

What Are You Focusing On?

The Family Eye of Time has four spheres of vision: near focus, far focus, peripheral vision and blind spots.

In our near focus are activities that we can't help but focus on because they're right in front of us. As parents, quite often our near focus is overwhelmed with chores and mundane, humdrum things that swamp us. Things like cooking, cleaning and working. Watching TV is a real favourite in many people's near focus. Did you know that mums spend about ten hours a week cleaning and tidying up?

In far focus are things we're aware of, but don't focus on. For example, if the children are watching TV and you're doing the ironing, the children are in your far focus and the ironing is in your near focus.

Peripheral vision captures things that you know are there, but you can only see from the corner of your eye. There's not such an awareness of them. In the illustration overleaf, we can see that family days out or cycling trips are in the peripheral vision sphere. Quite often things sit in that sphere of vision because day-to-day things have taken over your near focus.

In the blind spots are activities that you just don't see any more. How many of us say we'll go for a weekend camping, or go on a family walk or spend more time helping with homework, but then never get round to doing them? We put them off for so long that eventually we forget about them and they move into our mental blind spots. In this example the family days out are in danger of moving from peripheral vision into a blind spot. Think for a moment about the things you want to spend time doing with your children but don't. These are in your peripheral vision. What about things you've forgotten about or perhaps have left for so long that your children are too old to do them now? These are your blind-spot activities.

Take a look at the Family Eye of Time and see what's in the different spheres of vision for this family.

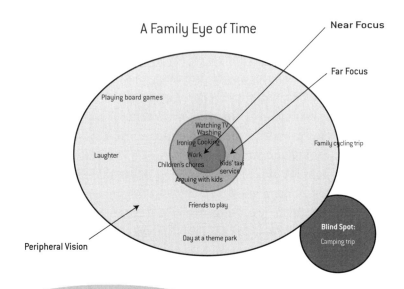

A Family Eye of Time

Near Focus

Far Focus

Playing board games

Watching TV
Washing
Ironing Cooking
Work
Children's chores   Kids' taxi
service
Arguing with kids

Family cycling trip

Laughter

Friends to play

Blind Spot:
Camping trip

Day at a theme park

Peripheral Vision

From the Mouths of Mums

*I really love reading my daughter a bedtime story. I know
it sounds ridiculous but when I get home and do that, I
feel like I'm being a good parent. To me the bedtime story
is real quality time. The problem is, other things at work
always seem to get in the way and hold me up. They come
into my near focus and the story often falls out of focus into
my peripheral vision.*

My Time Audit

The second Truth of Time Management is this: 'To save time,
you must first know how you spend it.' So, using the Family
Eye of Time, think about what kind of activities you focus on
now. How are you spending your time? What's in your near
focus? What's in your far focus? What's in your peripheral
vision and what's fallen into your blind spot? Where's that
place or what's that activity that you keep promising you'll

take the children to but never get round to? Perhaps a day out cycling is something you've often thought about doing, but it's in your blind spot. Perhaps most of your near-focus activities with the children are things like homework, or do you spend too much time nagging in that sphere? Whatever your reality is, write it down, using the blank Family Eye of Time (below or on page 224), or draw one of your own.

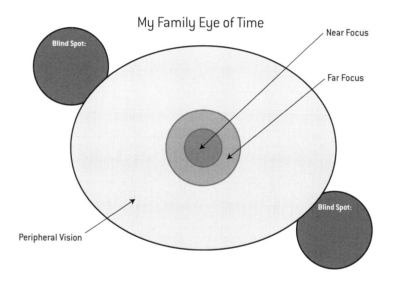

My Family Eye of Time

If you want to get even greater clarity on what your Family Eye of Time looks like, then why not try doing a family time audit for the next week? This will really get you thinking about and tuned in to where you focus your time. Make a copy of the log overleaf or use the one on page 226 and fill it out as you go along this week to get a more accurate picture of what's in your focus most of the time.

Tip! Think ahead. Each day, imagine your long-term future: what will the consequences of your actions be?

Family Quality Time Audit
Keep a record of your day by noting each new activity you start and how long it lasts. If you are with your children, notice how focused or distracted you are. Do it as you go along; that way you get a much more accurate picture.

Time activity started	Activity	Did this activity involve my family?	How am I feeling? What is my mental, emotional, physical state (tired, stressed, distracted, happy)? How focused am I?	Duration in minutes

From the Mouths of Mums

It wasn't until I really analysed where I spent my time that I realized not enough of it was with my children. I'd always thought I should spend more time with them, but I didn't realize just how distracted I was when I was with them. It made me realize that if I wanted to get on with them better I had to spend more time with them and try to be more focused when I did.

When you've got your week's worth of data, just add up how many of your minutes you spent on family activities, when you felt focused and when both you and the children were enjoying it. It's usually quite an eye-opener.

Now you know what your time profile looks like, you can begin to change it into the profile that you want.

What Does Quality Time Mean to You?

Time Management's third Truth I find compelling: 'Know what you want, then you'll find time to look for it.' So, if the Family Eye of Time you just drew up isn't what you want to see, get clear in your mind what you'd *like* it to look like instead. In other words, *know what you want*. Being able to articulate exactly what you'd like to be doing with your time takes you halfway to achieving it. So, what do you want? Use the Family Eye of Time to help you find out.

Your ideal Family Eye of Time

Draw up your ideal Family Eye of Time (overleaf or on page 225), placing things you'd like to focus on in the centre, and things you don't want to focus on in a blind spot. What would be in your near and far focus if you were spending quality time with your children? What would come out of your blind spot? Now, you might not be able to do all these things all at once, but recognizing that you want them in your near focus at some point is crucial.

From the Mouths of Mums

I realized that as my children got older they would probably want to spend less and less time with me, as I became increasingly uncool! So it became really important to me to find an activity that we could all do together as a family. We all joined the tennis club. I'd not played since school and was awful, but took lessons and began to improve.

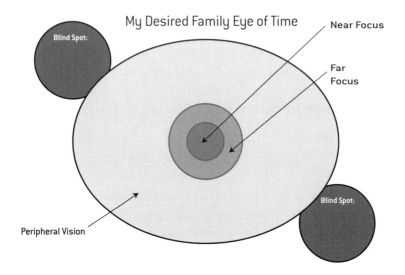

My Desired Family Eye of Time

Near Focus

Far Focus

Blind Spot:

Blind Spot:

Peripheral Vision

The children also took lessons and now as a family we play tennis socially. The children can go on their own and play with friends. It's been a brilliant plan. It's pulled us together but also allows the children to be independent.

Turning the Plan into Reality

So, this is all great, but how do you manage to get round to doing all these activities? Most of us lead lives that are so full we can barely squeeze in what has to be done in a day, let alone anything extra. To help you solve the perennial problem of how you find enough time to fit in the activities that you'd really like to do with your family, I'd like to introduce you to Truth Four: 'Take control of time or time will take control of you.'

Once you know what you want, why not take control and make it happen? Most of us feel better when we're in control. If you think about times when you've felt stressed, it's probably mostly been when you've felt you had little or no control. Taking control is the key to getting things done.

I'd like to give you a couple of tools to help you get all the control you need. The first is the 'Wine Bottle Theory of Time Management'. Daft as it sounds, it's a theory that will help you to think about how you prioritize your time, and achieve the things that will really add value to your life. These are often the things we neglect, like quality time with our family.

Gathering the ingredients

Let's break the theory down into a few easily digestible morsels so that you can instantly understand it and begin to get the benefits.

Step One
As with any great recipe for success, you need to assemble a few key ingredients:

☆ a wine carafe (if, like me, you're not that posh and you don't have one, worry not: a plastic jug will do)
☆ an open bottle of wine (tricky, I know, but full of wine, please)
☆ a bag of apples
☆ a carton of blueberries
☆ a bag of caster sugar.

An odd mêlée of ingredients, I agree, but just you wait and see what magic we're going to do with them. These ingredients symbolize the different aspects of your day. Imagine that the jug is your day as a whole, while all the empty space in it represents the individual hours, minutes and seconds of your day. On any given day you will endeavour to get as many tasks done as possible. So the object of the exercise is to do exactly the same with the jug, and squeeze in as much as you can. The apples, blueberries, caster sugar and wine represent all the tasks you have to do. Your challenge is to fill the jug to the brim with them. Faced with an empty jug, how do you get the maximum amount in? What do you put in first, the apples, blueberries, caster sugar or wine? Progress to step two and you'll find out.

Step Two
Put as many apples as you can into the jug so it's full to the top with apples and there is no room for any more. The jug is full – or is it?

Step Three
Put as many blueberries as you can in the jug. They should fit in around the apples, filling up the smaller gaps. Do this until the jug looks full and there is no room for any more blueberries. The jug is full – or is it?

Step Four
Take the caster sugar and pour in as much as you can until, once again, the jug looks full and there is no room for any more caster sugar. The jug is completely and utterly full to the top – or is it?

Step Five
Although it really will look full now, don't be deceived. Take your bottle of wine and pour some in. As you do this, remember, this experiment is in the interests of science, your sanity and personal development. Try not to think too much about the fact that you could actually be drinking it! Unbelievably, as it trickles into the jug there will still be some very small spaces that the liquid is able to fill. You may even be surprised by how much wine the jug can take (like you after a hard day at work or being driven mad by the kids!). Keep going until the jug is full to capacity and, to get any more in, you would need to get another jug, or a new day.

Step Six

Stand back and look in amazement at how much you've been able to fit easily into the jug. Avoid thinking about what a horrible sticky mess it's going to be to clean up, just look on in wonderment.

Step Seven

Ponder for a moment how this little exercise might revolutionize your life. For most of us, the jug that represents our day gets too full, too quickly. We often find ourselves at the end of the day with a pile of leftover ingredients sitting next to the jug. Without exception I find this to be the case. Parents find their jug gets too full, too quickly, with things that aren't what they really wanted in there in the first place. Why?

Be a 'Wine-no'

Well, you don't need a degree in rocket science to realize that what we did here was to put the big things in first and then the progressively smaller and smaller things, until the jug was filled to the top. To get the maximum amount into your jug, you must start with the apples. Do it any other way and you get fewer apples in, or no apples at all. 'But why,' I hear you cry, 'why put the apples in first?'

The apples in your jug represent the most important things that you have to do in your day. If you don't do these, then your world will fall apart. They have to be tackled right there and then. Your tax return has to be in tomorrow or you'll be fined. This would be an apple.

> *Tip!* Have a family meeting each week. Discuss issues that are important to the family. Ensure everybody has the opportunity to talk about anything that's worrying them, and that they are listened to by other family members.

The blueberries represent the tasks that are your lesser priorities that day. These can fit in around the apples. They're the items that you want to appear in your near focus, but you always endeavour to find a way of tackling your apple tasks first.

The caster sugar represents those tasks that you want in your far focus until you are ready to do them, i.e. when you've done the more important things. I'm thinking here of things like social telephone calls.

Wine represents the most low-grade tasks you have on your list, the fluff, the filler, the things you do only when everything else has been completed. A 20-minute chat in the playground with the other mums after you've dropped the children off would be a wine activity. If you're anything like me, given the choice of an apple, a blueberry, a spoonful of sugar or a glass of wine, there's no competition. You'll go for the wine every time. So often we do this in life.

When faced with a series of options, we go for the one that instantly gratifies us, rather than the one that doesn't immediately appeal, even if we know that it will provide us with a longer-term benefit. Faced with the choice of pain or pleasure, we choose pleasure. Well, come on, we are human. We tackle the vino first. We fill our jug to the brim with wine, and leave no room for the apples or the blueberries. When your jug is full of apples it's always possible to add some wine. Why not indulge in the playground chit-chat at the end of the day when you've got more time because you've done your more important apple, blueberry and caster sugar jobs in the morning. When your jug is full of wine, it's not possible to add anything, because it's full. There are no gaps, and the apples, the blueberries and the caster sugar remain untouched on the counter. They remain on your to-do list day after day, until eventually they disappear into a blind spot, never to be seen again. Sober up, put the wine down. Be a wine-no.

Tip! Notice what triggers annoyance, impatience or other unwanted behaviours in yourself. Ask yourself 'What do I need to do to remove these triggers?'

Child Alcohol Syndrome

Also, if you're filling your day with wine activities, what damage is this doing to your family? If, on the other hand, you're filling your day with fruit, it's got to be better. Time with your children is the equivalent of the apples and blueberries in your jug, and when you're going through your day the activities represented by the fruit should be your top priorities. Make sure you're getting your five a day! Whether it's planning something big or something small, ignore this wisdom and I'm fairly certain that you'll not get the juice and zest out of life with your children that you want. To really internalize the wisdom of this theory and get it into the muscle so it works for you and you stay at the top of the spiral, I suggest that every day you make a plan of activities that you want to do with your children. Let me give you an example of what I mean and how you would make it happen.

Making the Family Eye of Time reality

When you look at your Family Eye of Time, what stands out as something you really want to do, something that would enhance your family life but that you've not got round to doing yet? It's in your peripheral vision or a blind spot. The activity will either be a big thing that might take a bit of organization, or it will be a small thing that you could almost do straightaway. The key is that you bring it into near focus and consider how you can make it a reality.

Let's say there are two things you want to do. One might be spending 20 minutes a day playing games or doing something creative with each of your children. The other might be taking the family on a camping weekend. Both things are easy to put off, so make a plan to make them happen!

Plan for success

Each night, sit down for 12 minutes and plan. In this sacred time, decide exactly what you want to focus on the following day. Also include on your list all the other things you have to do, then prioritize the day. When you have your list, assign a priority to each item on it, giving each thing either an A, B, C or D. A items are like your apples, the activities you'll do first. Start giving the activities that often get pushed to one side a chance to get into the jug by assigning them A status. These might be things that have perhaps fallen victim to your blind spot. Tasks labelled B are your blueberries or the things you'll do second, C tasks are your caster sugar and you do these third. Ds are your wine. They are the last tasks that you'll tackle.

When assigning priorities, avoid falling into the urgency trap. Often we get distracted and consumed by urgencies in our day, tasks that we believe we have to do, but that aren't necessarily important in terms of their quality. Phone calls, texts, emails, a friend calls round, your boss asks you to stay late, the TV. It's quite hard to walk past a TV without watching, isn't it? We often give these 'urgencies' more of a priority than they deserve and, while doing that, we neglect the activities that are important to us because they don't grab our attention and make themselves urgent. Leave these things for too long and they have a habit of coming back to bite you on the bum. Let me give you an example of what I mean. I had a friend who told me she'd not written a will. Now, with children, having a will is pretty important, but in your 40s you hope it isn't that urgent. It became urgent for her, though, when she developed acute angina and was rushed to hospital. When we neglect valuable things, they have a habit of suddenly becoming urgent. By not attending to important tasks we run the risk of them coming into near focus when we least expect them to. Too many of these and we live in a world of stress where we are constantly fighting to keep on top of things. Take control.

Systems Save Time

Time Truth Five tells us that 'Systems save time.' Why not streamline your life and find efficient ways of managing the predicable, humdrum tasks you know you have to do every day? If you do, you'll suddenly find you have more time.

Freeing up time so we can spend quality moments that matter with our family can be tricky; there's just so much to do. Cooking, cleaning, washing, ironing – to name but a few – eat up our hours. It's like a production line. So why not use some of the best techniques from the world of mass production and put systems in place? They'll save you oodles of time and will help your house run more smoothly.

Systemize Cooking
If you went to a restaurant, do you think when he saw you coming, the chef would rummage through the freezer to see what he had in and hope for the best? How often have you foraged for a fish finger in the freezer at tea time, with no idea of what you might find? Probably more times that you care to remember. Mums spend between ten and 17 hours a week cooking and clearing up. Why not cut down on this and create a rolling menu? Plan your meals ahead of time, bulk buy, freeze, get a system in place. I promise it'll save you hours.

Systemize Shopping
With a rolling menu up and running, shopping becomes easy because you know what you need to buy. On average we spend between three and six hours a week shopping. Now,

I don't know about you, but I'd rather be doing something with my family. Don't shop till you drop, create a running shopping list that ties in with your rolling menu. Order your groceries over the Internet. Let someone else take the strain of shopping while you focus on your family.

Systemize Filing

How much time do you waste looking for bits of paper, information about school trips and medical appointments? Even worse, how many things have you missed because you lost the relevant pieces of information? Systemize your filing and you'll save time and aggro. Instead of using your fridge or the floor as filing systems, invest in a 31-day concertina folder to capture all your paper until you need it. Whenever paper enters your hand, ask yourself 'Should I do this, dump this or delegate this?' If you can do it right away, then just do it. If you can't and it needs to be done at a later date, put it into the 31-day folder on the day it will become relevant. Every day, look in your folder. Information and paper will appear on the day that you need it to. Start to really think about how you can organize the paper flow in your house so you don't waste time on it.

Systemize Cleaning

If you can't offload the cleaning on someone else, get a cleaning routine established. We spend about ten hours a week cleaning. Instead of dedicating a day to this activity, do it in small chunks. Write down all the cleaning jobs you want done and spread them out over the week or month. Use your 31-day divided folder or an electronic planner and assign tasks to a day. If it's a weekly task, like mopping the kitchen floor, when it's done move it forward to the next week. This way you'll keep on top of everything. To keep on top of monthly jobs, buy a 12-pocket folder to hold jobs you do less regularly, and look in this folder once a month.

Do two things at once. Can you clean the bath as part of the bathtime routine? You're a woman, you can multitask! Simple things like this make cleaning seem much more manageable. If you don't want to waste time removing mess and clutter, insist that your family follow the golden rule: 'Don't put it down, put it away.'

Systemize Kids
Getting routines going with your children is essential. Homework, bathtime, bedtime and getting ready in the morning are just a few for you to think about. Simple things like children putting out their own clothes the night before can be really helpful in the morning when every minute matters. Don't be afraid to get your children involved in household activities that will save you time, like cleaning their own shoes or making their own beds. You know how to negotiate and make agreements with them, so go for it.

Don't Put It Off!

In the words of Truth Six, 'The cost of putting things off is higher than the price of doing them.'

Our children fall into this category. They are valuable, but we can always put them off until tomorrow. Then one day we wake up and it's too late. Choose to focus on them while you can. Make it a priority. Ultimately you have a choice about what you focus on, and if playing with your children for 20 minutes is valuable to you, then choose to do that before something less important like the ironing. If it's really important to you, make that 20 minutes of playtime with the children a planned item on your daily list. Prioritize it; go as far as to schedule in the time when you'll do it. Perhaps between 4.00 and 4.20. This way it's more likely to happen. Honour the appointment in the same way you would if it were with a doctor, your boss or another adult.

Planning the bigger things in life

Sometimes we don't spend time doing things we'd like to because organizing them seems too big or onerous a task. We get caught up in the fray of family life and never get round to doing these special things. A camping trip is an example. It's not just a matter of fitting it in, but of organizing it well ahead of time. This is an activity that might slip into your peripheral vision and then fall into a blind spot. To help make time to do the bigger things in life, I like to use a technique called *chunking*.

Instead of thinking about tasks as huge and unmanageable, break them down into more palatable pieces. It's a bit like eating an apple. If someone gave you an apple, how would you eat it? Probably one bite at a time. You wouldn't try to put the whole thing in your mouth. When you take it bite by bite it's enjoyable and you're not going to choke as you shove it all in at once. Let's apply the idea of chunking to organizing a camping weekend. How would you find time to make that happen without it seeming to take any time at all?

The three Magic Questions

I use three Magic Questions to break down big tasks into smaller chunks or bites. Start by deciding *when* you would like to go on your camping weekend. Let's say it's in four months' time and that at the moment it's mid-January. So, you'd like to go in mid-April for a break at Easter. Then work backwards from the completion date to calculate what bites of your apple you need to take before then. The three Magic Questions that will help you work out all the information you need are:

1. What do I need to do?
2. When do I need to do it by?
3. What else do I need to do?

Tip! *If you're too tired, it's hard to be a great parent. Make sure you make time for yourself, too.*

So, in this example, the answer to 'What do I need to organize a family camping holiday?' will be: 'I need to find a campsite.'

Next ask Magic Question Two, 'By when do I have to complete the action?' In this case, let's say 3rd February. Note the answer as an action in your diary.

Now we come to Magic Question Three, 'What else do I need to do in order to organize the holiday?' The first answer that springs to mind might be 'Get hold of appropriate camping equipment.' This will lead you logically to the next question: 'What has to happen for me to get camping equipment?' Answer: 'I need to visit a camping shop to find out what I need.'

Give yourself a deadline: 'By when do I have to complete this action?' Let's say 20th February. Note this as an action in your diary. Other answers will include 'Book the Campsite,' 'Buy the tent,' etc. And so it goes on, until when you ask the question, 'What else do I need to do to organize a family camping holiday?' the answer is 'Nothing.' You have all your action steps and they are broken down in small, tangible chunks that you can tackle over a period of time. Instead of the camping weekend remaining in your blind spot, it will come into your near focus as small actions on a regular basis until it actually takes place in April.

Camping Weekend Steps	Due Date	Notes
Check what equipment we need; visit a camping shop.	20th January	
Book time off work.	25th January	
Buy equipment.	30th January	
Ask friends who have camped what and where they would recommend.	1st February	Spend 20 minutes on phone to three friends who have camped over a period of a week.
Research campsites.	3rd February	Spend three sessions of 30 minutes on the Internet looking for a campsite.
Book a campsite.	10th February	
Get a list of items to take with us.	28th February	Contact three friends who have camped; pick their brains.
Pack.	10th April	
Enjoy camping weekend.	15th April	

Where else can I find time to spend with my children?

Planning is a time-saving activity in its own right. Identifying what is important to you and getting that done first will give you a sense of control that's often lacking. But where else can you free up time? The truth is that you can't create more time, but you can be resourceful with what you've got and be aware of when you're not using it efficiently. Sometimes we let our time seep away without even noticing where it's gone. It's a bit like the water shortages we have encountered in the UK. Now, the UK is not renowned for drought-like conditions, but in the summer of 2006 we seemed subject to constant hosepipe bans because of water shortages. Why was this? Was it because we didn't have enough water? No, we had more than enough; just look at our rainfall! The shortage was caused by leaky pipes. The pipes that deliver the water from the reservoirs to our taps are full of holes. En route to our houses, gallons and gallons of water are lost. It just seeps away. Time is the same: we let it leak out of our day. If you were to analyse your week or day, where would your leaks be? Where do you regularly lose time? What activities waste your time? Here're a few common time-robbers:

1. chatting in the playground
2. constant trips to the shops for forgotten items
3. queuing
4. arguing with children about doing their chores/home-work
5. picking up things that people have dropped
6. surfing the Internet
7. getting distracted from the job in hand so it takes much longer
8. unnecessary phone calls
9. constant coffee breaks
10. not preparing things in advance
11. poor filing and information-retrieval systems
12. texting and emailing
13. reading the paper
14. watching TV
15. saying 'Yes' when you should say 'No.'

An exercise in making quality time

If you want to bring into focus the items on your Ideal Family Eye, eliminating your time-wasters could help you to claw back lost seconds, minutes and hours. Think of three things that waste at least ten minutes of your day, every day. Eliminate them from your life and immediately you've got 30 minutes. What have you put on your Family Eye of Time as something you'd like in near focus that takes 30 minutes to do? Choose to do that instead.

The Pinnacle: Enjoying Every Moment of Motherhood

With your life licked into shape, you're now in a position to enjoy every minute of it. But do you sometimes find that time seems to run away with you? Does one day roll into the next? Do you sometimes struggle to remember what you did last week? Is life just a blur? Have you ever got to the end of the six-week summer holidays wondering where they went? In July they seemed to stretch endlessly before you. Then suddenly, in a flash they're over. Summer has gone and the autumn has arrived. 'It'll soon be Christmas,' you mutter to yourself as you drop off the children for the new academic year. Do you ever wish you could slow time down and savour it more? Well, you'll be pleased to hear that you can. Time Truth Seven states that 'If you can live in the moment, you can expand time.' So how do you live in the moment and enjoy every single one of them? Well, there are a few things you can do.

Golden events

A great way of savouring time is to punctuate it with what I call 'golden events'. The reason time sometimes seems to drag when you're in it but feels like it went quickly when you look back is that often there's not much to separate one day from the next in your memory. If all you do is hum-drum activities like cooking, cleaning and nagging, one day will just roll into another. It's like painting a wall one colour:

it's bland and uninteresting, there's not much to differentiate one part of the wall from the other. By creating memorable events and family traditions that punctuate your past memories, you spice up your life and add a splash of colour to the canvas of your family memory bank. This will appear to slow time down.

Why not create family traditions that your children will remember and share with their own children? These events act like the punctuation in a sentence: they stop one word rolling into the next so everything makes sense.

Why not involve the whole family in this process? Get their opinions on what they'd like to be doing. To get more clarity on this, ask your family what golden events they'd like to see coming into near focus. You now have all the skills you need to request, negotiate, listen and accommodate what you all want. Add their requests to your Family Eye of Time.

Take time to savour and plan your year. At the start of a year, ask 'What can we do as a family, or as individuals, that will help this year to stand out?' As I write this, it's January. My family and I have sat down to plan all the fun things we'd like to do this year. Punctuating the year with golden events will give the illusion of elongating the year; when you look back on it, there will be something to see. Make things stand out even more by reflecting on what you've done over the year. Do you have your family photos and video footage sorted in any meaningful way? Have a family evening sorting out photos. What a wonderful way to savour what you've been up to.

The Right State or a Right State?

If you want to enjoy every minute with your children, you've got to be in the right state to do it, rather than in a right state. If you find it hard to concentrate on your children because your mind is elsewhere, try these strategies to help.

Buffer Time and Early Delivery

If you're always in a rush it's hard to enjoy fully what you're doing because you're in a state of stress. Try the simple technique of allowing yourself some 'buffer time'. Don't leave things until the last minute. Try to arrive everywhere five minutes early, and see what a difference that makes to your stress levels and interactions with your children. If George has a piece of homework to complete, bring the deadline forward. Do it when you've got time, not when you're in a rush. This has an amazing impact on the way your children experience you. You'll seem different to them when you're calm and in control.

Focus

To make the most of your time with your children, it's great if you can focus when you're with them. If your mind's on what you're going to have for tea or you're mentally mulling over last night's episode of *Desperate Housewives*, it's hard to enjoy the moment. How much time do you spend wishing away the next stage of your children's or even your own life? With the pace of life as it is, sometimes it feels that having a family is like being on an express train. We whiz along on our journey, not able to stop and savour the countryside. A recent holiday on a barge really brought home to me the value of slowing down and taking time to enjoy the simple things in life. As we chugged away at two mph – the top speed of our handsome vessel – I read a sign: 'The only way to speed up is to slow down.' How true, I thought, and what a wonderful thing to ponder as a piece of advice for our own lives.

Mental Boundaries

If you find it hard to focus on what you're doing with your family because your mind's on your work, then you're not alone. It's a common problem. If you need to have your BlackBerry surgically removed from your hand before you can make Luke Skywalker in Lego with your son, you're unlikely to savour the moment. (What do you mean, you're very good at left-handed Lego?) Set up some mental boundaries. When you leave work, perhaps the door of the office building could be a sign to you that you're going home. It's time to switch into 'home mode'. When you walk through your front door, remind yourself that you're *home*. If you're accessible by email and mobile in the evening, resist the temptation to keep looking at and answering them. Your children will wait until tomorrow, but so will work. Ask yourself the question – and answer it honestly – which is more vital to your life, and which one can't survive without you? Then make your choice. If you're worried your world will fall apart, just try it for a few days. Notice what happens to you and your kids.

Mind Your Language

We often speak in the language of 'rush'. It's almost as if it's trendy to be in a hurry. How often have you said things like:

'I'm just so busy at the moment.'

'I don't know where my day goes.'

'I never have a minute to myself.'

'Where does the time go?'

'Time just flies.'

Try to eliminate phrases such as these from your vocabulary. If you say them often enough, you begin to believe them. If you hear yourself using the language of rush, say something more empowering instead:

'I rush from one thing to the next' becomes 'I used to rush from one thing to the next, but I'm not like that any more.'

Time is the greatest gift we have. It's also the greatest gift we can give to our children. Quality time is the pinnacle of life, and it's the pinnacle of family life. Follow the wisdom of the Seven Truths of Time Management and you'll get more of it. By choosing to value your time and creating clear family goals, you can start to take control of your time. By planning and organizing, you'll get more done faster, leaving you time for the things you really want to do. Many might say they haven't got time to do it. My view: with fewer than 50,000 one-on-one hours with your children, you haven't got time not to.

Summary

☆ Everybody wants more time to spend with their family. Unfortunately, there is no more time.

☆ It's important to get clear about what we spend our time on and what we would rather spend our time on.

☆ When we know what we want from our time with our children, we can begin to plan how we will achieve it.

☆ We can gain more time by noticing where we lose it and beginning to claim it back.

☆ When we learn to focus we can more readily savour the time we have with our children.

Week Seven Actions

☆ Complete your current and your ideal Family Eye of Time.

☆ Make a plan so that you can begin to take action towards making your ideal Family Eye of Time a reality.

☆ Focus on enjoying all the hours, minutes and seconds you spend with your children, this week and for the rest of your life.

Afterword

Dear Allison,

Thanks so much for the upward spiral. As you suggested, each week I tried something new and things just got better and better. I now realize that I alone am in control of my emotions. How I behave with my children is entirely up to me. I've discovered that when I change my behaviour, the behaviour of my children changes, too. I have the power to become more magnetic.

Everyone has commented on how much more calm and relaxed I seem. Focusing on what's going right instead of what's going wrong has given me a more sunny outlook, and I'm definitely feeling magnificent, not manic. My children are arguing less. Just having the tools to talk, listen to and understand them has been a major help in improving their co-operation. We have agreements, not arguments, about who will do what and when. My son even takes out and brings in the dustbins without me having to nag any more. It's nothing short of a miracle. We're all getting on much better and we're now looking forward to more family outings, which includes a whole host of things that the children want to do. Thank you for sharing the success spiral – it works.

Yours,

A Magnificent Mum

Blank for you to write on:

My Current Family Eye of Time

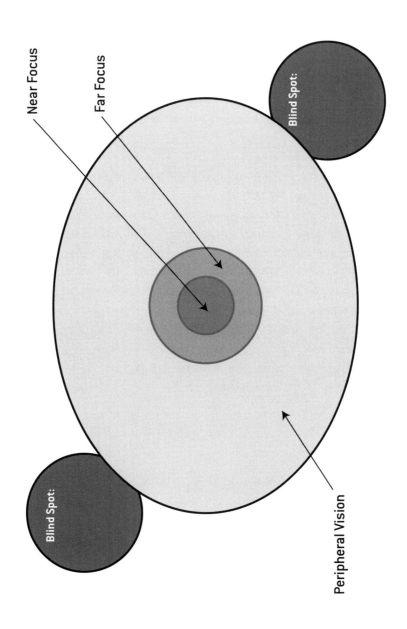

Blank for you to write on:

My Desired Family Eye of Time

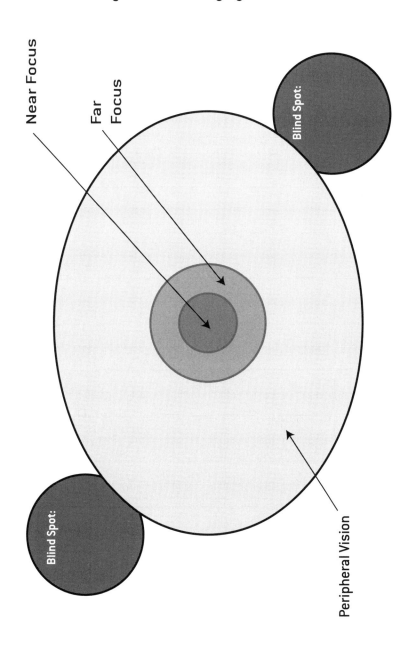

Family Quality Time Audit

Keep a record of your day by noting each new activity you start and how long it lasts. If you are with your children, notice how focused or distracted you are. Do it as you go along; that way you get a much more accurate picture.

Time activity started	Activity	Did this activity involve my family?	How am I feeling? What is my mental, emotional, physical state (tired, stressed, distracted, happy)? How focused am I?	Duration in minutes

Parent Coaching. Bring out your true brilliance

+mums
dads

Want to find out more about:
Seminars

•

Corporate workshops and talks

•

One-to-one coaching?

Then visit
www.mumcoach.com

If you'd like Allison to speak at an event call
0870 4603670

Hay house titles of related interest

YOU CAN HEAL YOUR LIFE, the movie,
starring Louise L. Hay & Friends
(available as a 1-DVD set and an expanded 2-DVD set)
Watch the trailer at www.LouiseHayMovie.com

*****

The Bloke's Guide to Babies, by Jon Smith
How to Be a Great Single Dad, by Theo Theobald
How to Stop Your Kids Watching too Much TV,
by Teresa Orange and Louise O'Flynn
Time Management for Manic Mums, by Allison Mitchell
You Can Have What You Want, by Michael Neill
You Can Heal Your Life, by Louise L. Hay

HAY HOUSE PUBLISHERS

Your Essential Life Companions

For the most up-to-date
information on the
latest releases, author
appearances and a host
of special offers, visit

www.hayhouse.co.uk

Tune into **www.hayhouseradio.com**
to hear inspiring live radio shows daily!

292B Kensal Rd, London W10 5BE
Tel: 020 8962 1230 Email: info@hayhouse.co.uk

We hope you enjoyed this Hay House book.
If you would like to receive a free catalogue featuring additional
Hay House books and products, or if you would like information
about the Hay Foundation, please contact:

Hay House UK Ltd
292B Kensal Rd • London W10 5BE
Tel: (44) 20 8962 1230; Fax: (44) 20 8962 1239
www.hayhouse.co.uk

✳✳✳

Published and distributed in the United States of America by:
Hay House, Inc. • PO Box 5100 • Carlsbad, CA 92018-5100
Tel.: (1) 760 431 7695 or (1) 800 654 5126;
Fax: (1) 760 431 6948 or (1) 800 650 5115
www.hayhouse.com

Published and distributed in Australia by:
Hay House Australia Ltd • 18/36 Ralph St • Alexandria NSW 2015
Tel.: (61) 2 9669 4299; Fax: (61) 2 9669 4144
www.hayhouse.com.au

Published and distributed in the Republic of South Africa by:
Hay House SA (Pty) Ltd • PO Box 990 • Witkoppen 2068
Tel./Fax: (27) 11 467 8904 • www.hayhouse.co.za

Published and distributed in India by:
Hay House Publishers India • Muskaan Complex • Plot No.3
B-2 • Vasant Kunj • New Delhi – 110 070.
Tel.: (91) 11 41761620; Fax: (91) 11 41761630.
www.hayhouse.co.in

Distributed in Canada by:
Raincoast • 9050 Shaughnessy St • Vancouver, BC V6P 6E5
Tel.: (1) 604 323 7100; Fax: (1) 604 323 2600

✳✳✳

Sign up via the Hay House UK website to receive the Hay House
online newsletter and stay informed about what's going on with
your favourite authors. You'll receive bimonthly announcements
about discounts and offers, special events, product highlights,
free excerpts, giveaways, and more!
www.hayhouse.co.uk